Drawing on History:
Abraham Lincoln

Text and illustrations copyright 2010 by Lee P. Sauer
All rights reserved.
Printed in the United States
ISBN: 978-0-578-04936-6

Second edition, June 2012

Summary: Lessons in drawing
from the life and times of
Abraham Lincoln.

To order copies of *Drawing on History: Abraham Lincoln*
and other C&C Press publications,
call (260) 665-1988
visit www.drawingsmiles.com
or send an email to drawingsmiles@yahoo.com.

*To Barb and Dick
for their love and support*

Getting Started

What this book is about
This book is part of a series called *Drawing on History*. Books in the series use history to teach drawing.

This is the first book in the series. The subject is Abraham Lincoln. Drawings are taken from the life of Abe. This book will show how to draw Abe, trees, a log cabin, critters and other things. And this book will teach facts about Abe's life.

Ready? Let's get started!

Lincoln's life
- Born February 12, 1809
- Married Mary Todd Nov. 4, 1842
- Father of four sons
- Elected 16th United States President November 1860
- Kept United States together through Civil War 1860-1865
- Freed United States slaves 1863
- Elected again November 1864
- Died April 15, 1865

Many people think Abe is the best president in United States history!

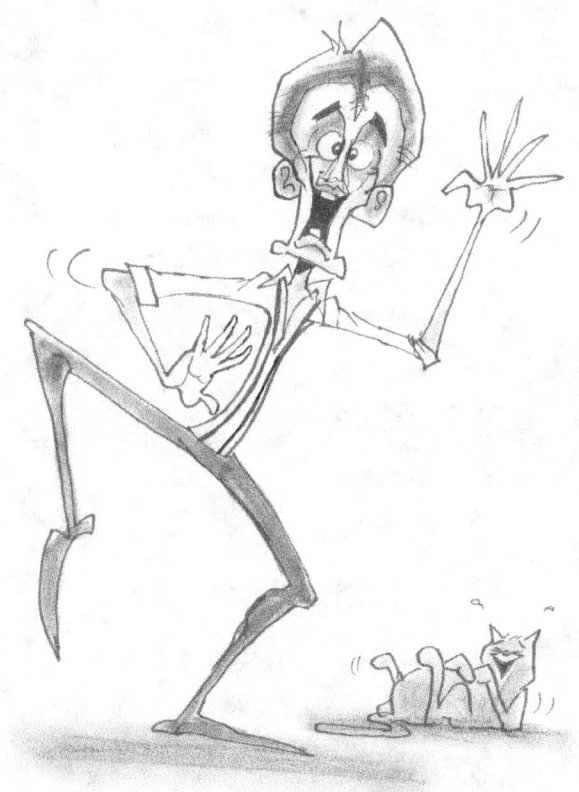

Storyteller—Abe loved to tell stories. He was good at it. People said Abe could make a cat laugh.

Drawing Tools

Tools for drawing are simple—paper and a pencil. Any paper will work. Copier paper. Computer paper. The back of a letter. An old envelope. A dirty napkin. (But not *too* dirty.) The pencil may be any type, too. A regular school pencil works great. And a nice, soft eraser will be useful. (Even the best artists make mistakes.)

But you can buy real artist tools. And the tools will not cost much. The tools used to make drawings in this book cost less than $20. The tools can be bought in an art store, or shop at www.dick-blick.com or www.cheapjoes.com.

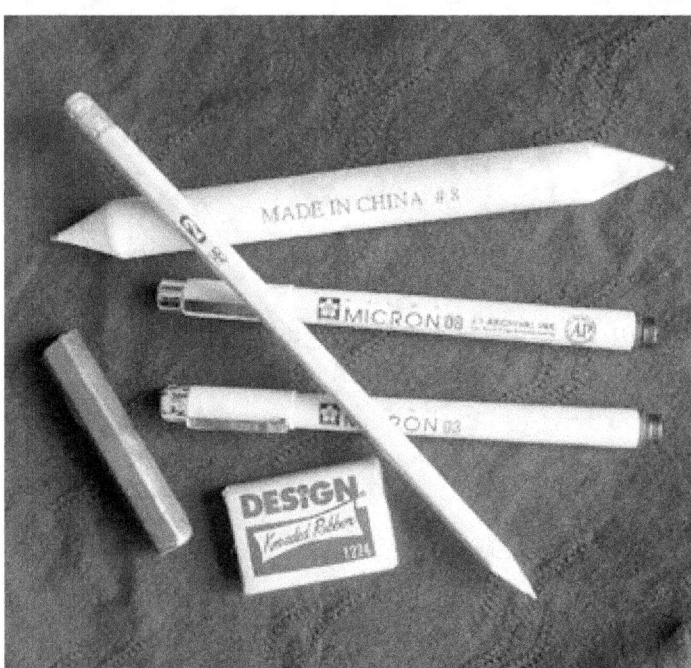

What to buy

- #2 pencil
- Pigma Micron .08 archival ink pen
- Pigma Micron .03 archival ink pen
- Design kneaded rubber eraser
- Lyra Graphite Crayon 1771 6B
- No. 8 blending stump
- Recycled, 20 lb. copier paper

How to use the tools

1. Sketch in pencil.
2. Trace over sketch with ink pens. The .08 makes thick lines. The .03 makes thin lines.
3. Clean up the drawing with the kneaded eraser.
4. Add shade with graphite crayon. Rub over the graphite with the blending stump.

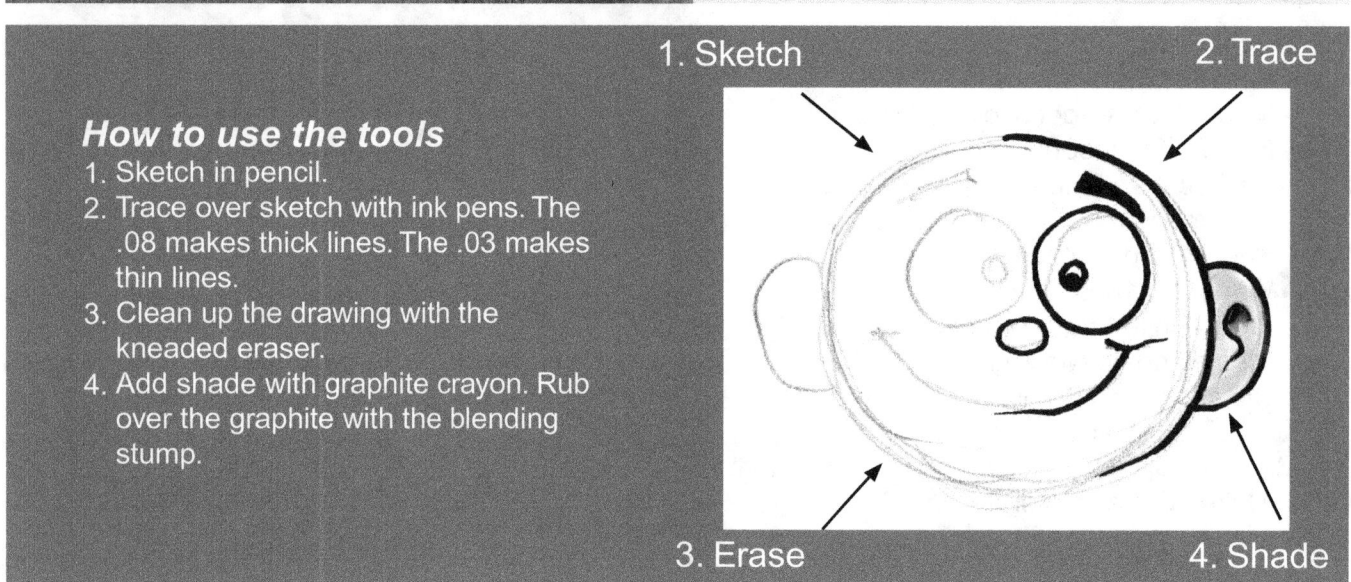

1. Sketch   2. Trace   3. Erase   4. Shade

Cartoons and caricatures

Cartoons are simple, funny drawings. An artist may draw a cartoon of anything. We will draw cartoon trees, rocks, hills, animals and people. Cartoons are fun and easy to draw.

A *caricature* is a cartoon, but it is special. A caricature is a simple, funny drawing of a real person. A good caricature looks like the person. A great caricature looks like the person and makes us laugh.

Long Abe Lincoln

Abe stood 6-foot-4. He would stand tall today. He stood very tall in his time.

Abe liked being tall. He wore a high hat to make himself even taller.

People called the hat a *stovepipe hat*. The hat was black. It looked like a pipe on a stove.

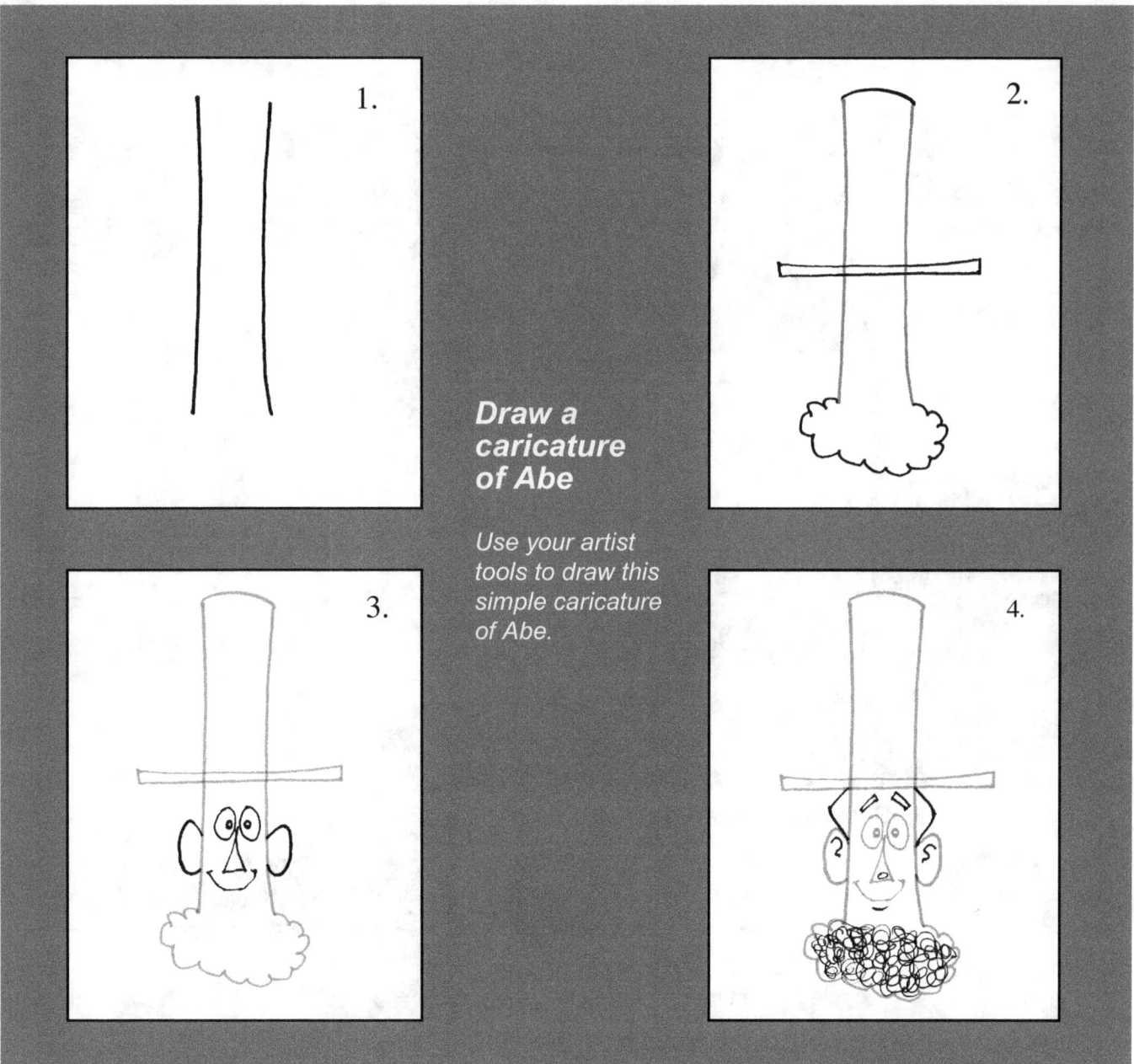

Draw a caricature of Abe

Use your artist tools to draw this simple caricature of Abe.

Shading

Our caricature of Old Abe looks good. It would look better shaded. Shade makes areas of dark, light and in-between. Shade brings drawings to life.

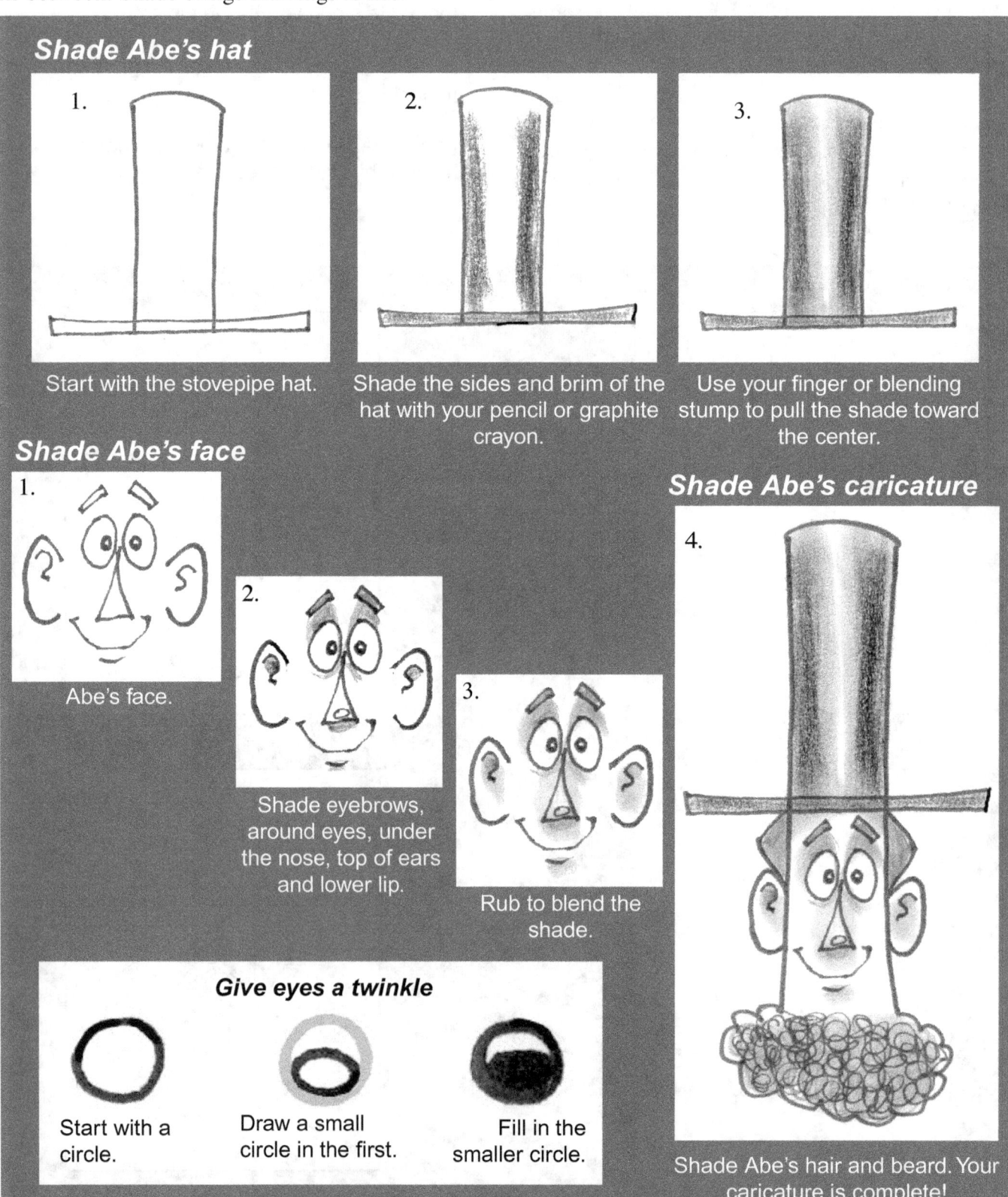

Shade Abe's hat

1. Start with the stovepipe hat.

2. Shade the sides and brim of the hat with your pencil or graphite crayon.

3. Use your finger or blending stump to pull the shade toward the center.

Shade Abe's face

1. Abe's face.

2. Shade eyebrows, around eyes, under the nose, top of ears and lower lip.

3. Rub to blend the shade.

Give eyes a twinkle

Start with a circle.

Draw a small circle in the first.

Fill in the smaller circle.

Shade Abe's caricature

4. Shade Abe's hair and beard. Your caricature is complete!

Sketching

Artists begin a drawing with a sketch. A sketch begins in the artist's eyes. It goes through the artist's mind and comes out of the artist's pencil. A sketch turns ideas into lines on paper.

Sketch test

With your pencil, sketch this steam engine. Do not worry if you struggle. This is only a test!

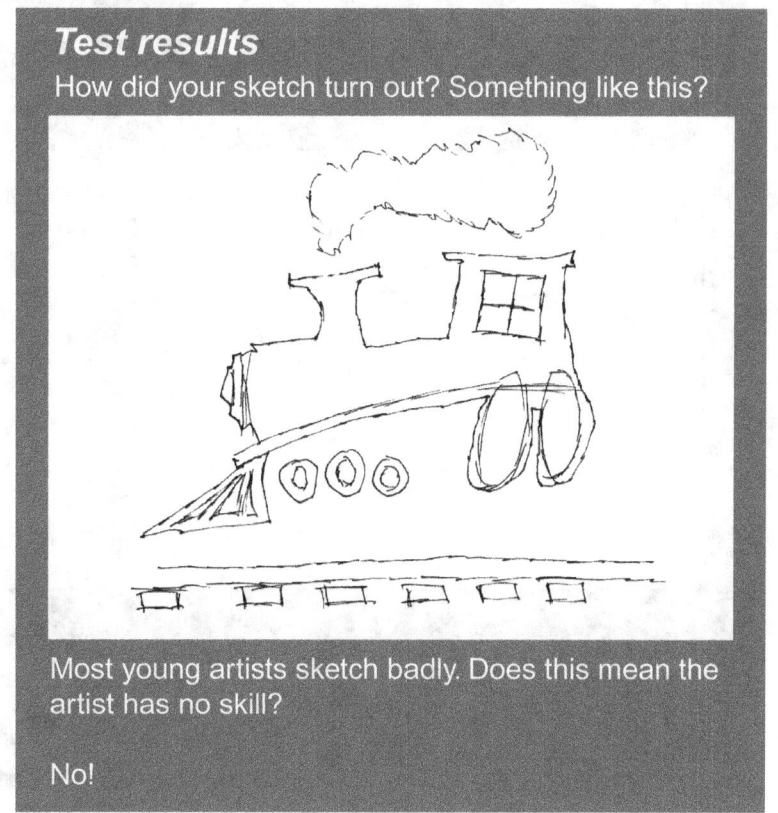

Abe and trains

Abe grew up with trains.

When Abe was born, there were no trains in the United States. When Abe became president, train tracks crossed the eastern part of the United States.

- 1804 First full-size steam locomotive built in England
- 1809 Abe born
- 1825 First American locomotive built
- 1860 Abe elected president

Do you know what year a train first came to your town?

Young artists look at a WHOLE subject. They see all the details. The eye-to-hand-to-paper path gets busy. It is like many trains on the same track. *Look out!*

When the mind gets busy, artists use careful lines. They try not to make mistakes. They erase often. This type of sketching is no fun. And the results are no good.

There's an easier way . . .

Test results

How did your sketch turn out? Something like this?

Most young artists sketch badly. Does this mean the artist has no skill?

No!

The secret of simple shapes

Artists have a secret way of looking at a subject. The secret frees the mind and makes sketching fun. The secret is simple, yet works like magic.

The secret is this: look for simple shapes.

You can draw a square, right? And a triangle? And a circle? When you look at a subject, see it as simple shapes. Look for squares and rectangles. Look for triangles. Look for circles and ovals.

To see simple shapes, ignore details. If it helps, squint your eyes. This will make the object fuzzy. Details will be out of focus.

Sketch one shape at a time. As you add shapes, your object will appear. Sketching simple shapes makes drawing easier. The secret of simple shapes works like magic!

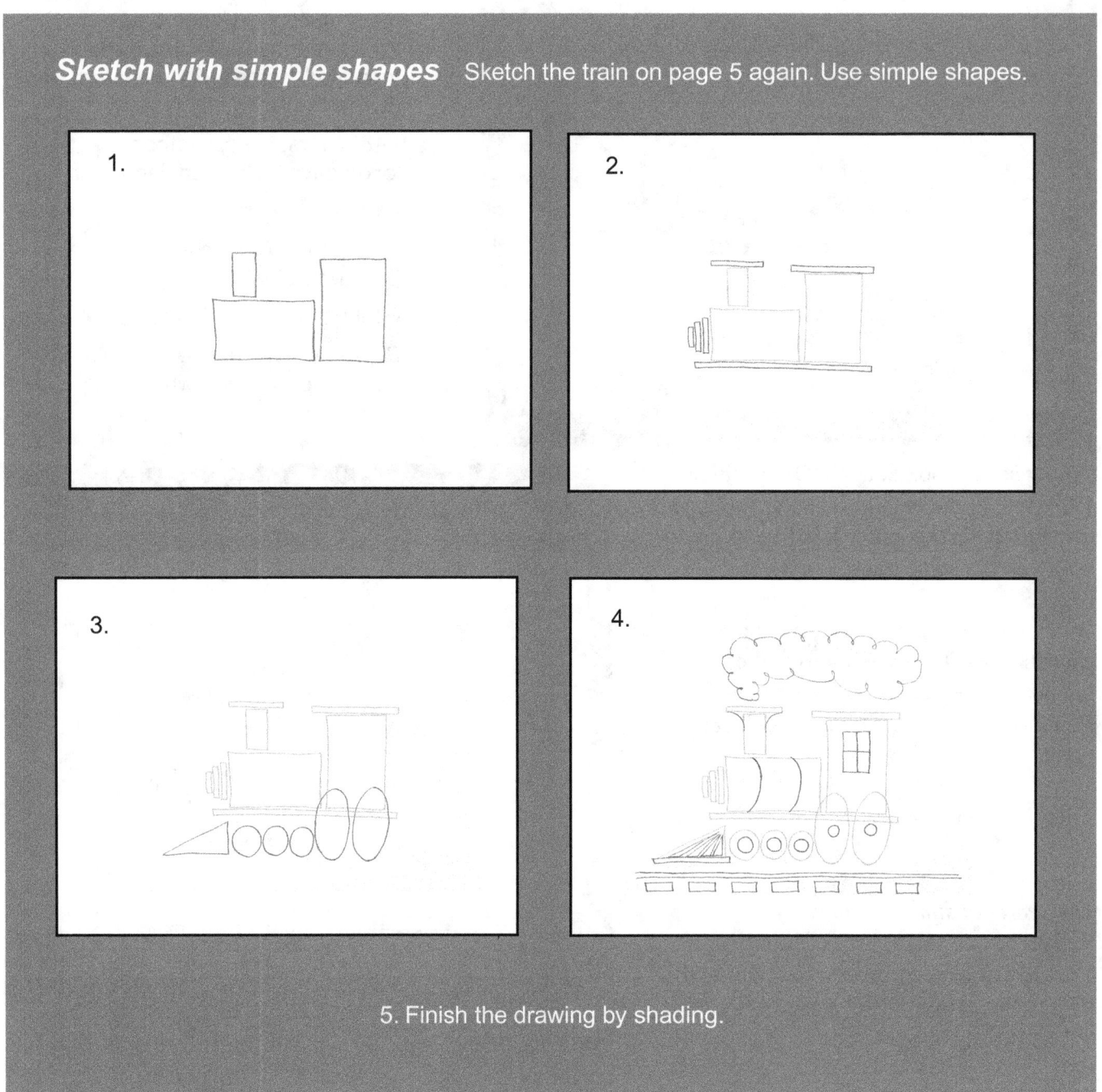

Sketch with simple shapes   Sketch the train on page 5 again. Use simple shapes.

1.

2.

3.

4.

5. Finish the drawing by shading.

Abe's Background

Back in Time

A background is the drawing behind the action. Think of your drawing as a play. In a play, actors perform on a stage. Your cartoon characters are actors. The background drawing is the stage.

What would we find in the background of Abe's childhood? To find out, we need to travel back in time.

Trees

Abe moved across the Ohio River in 1816. That year, Indiana became a state.

In 1816 trees covered a big part of the United States. One forest stretched from the Atlantic Ocean to Indiana. In Indiana, the forest stopped and the prairie began.

Pioneers told a story about a squirrel. It went from ocean to prairie without touching the ground. How? By jumping from tree to tree.

Look at a map of the United States. Find the Atlantic Ocean, the Ohio River and Indiana.

Draw tree-covered hills

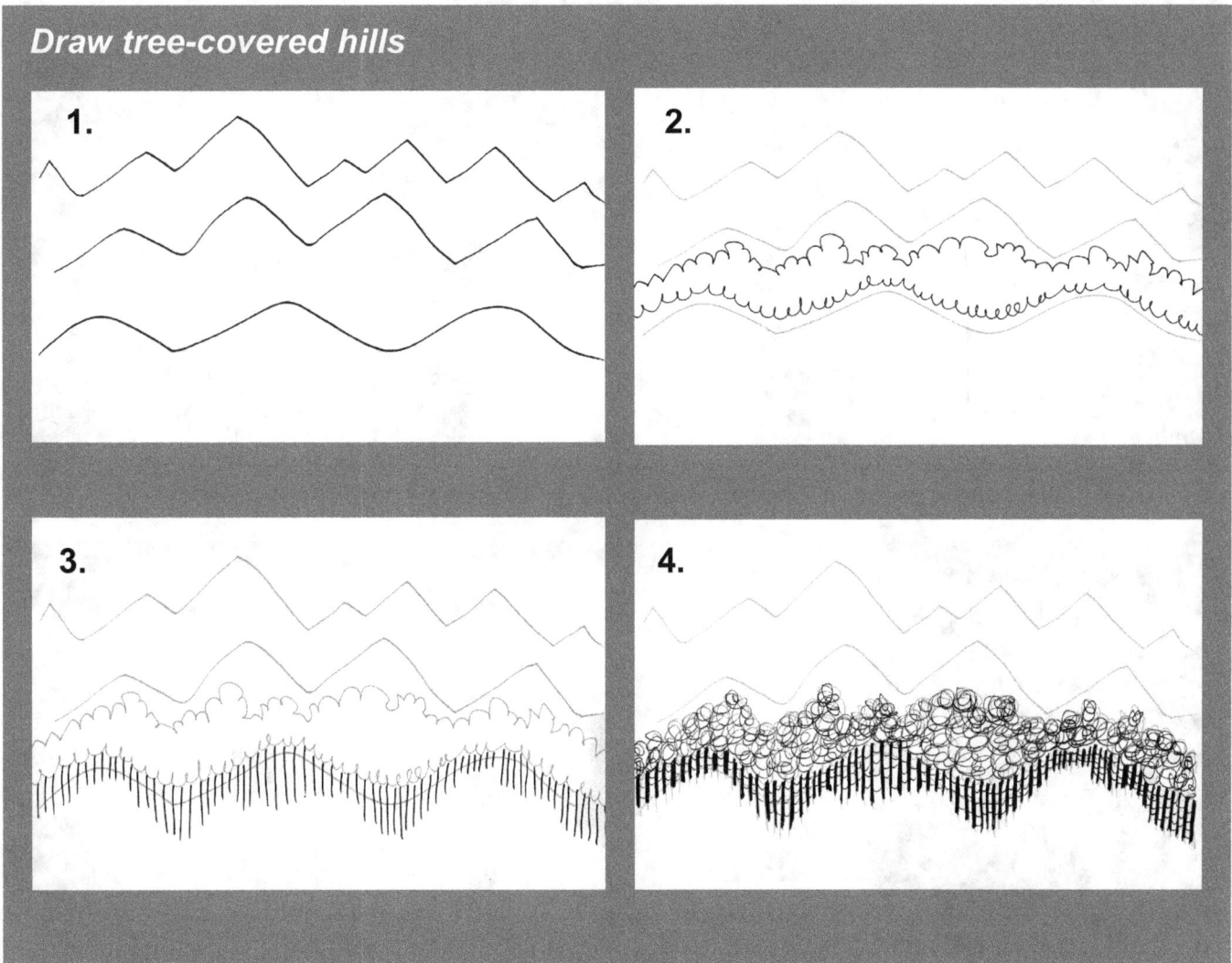

Living off the land

Imagine you are a pioneer. You live on the edge of the frontier. There are no stores. No roads. No hospitals. You do not have neighbors. You cannot hire workers. Police cannot protect you. Firefighters cannot save your home. You are on your own.

Pioneers had to find food. They had to make clothing and shelter. Pioneers brought a few things with them, but most things came from the land around them.

Pioneers on the frontier

When Abe was born, Americans lived along the Atlantic Ocean. To move west meant climbing mountains. It meant fighting. (Native Americans, the French, and British felt Americans had enough land.)

But Americans were like spilled milk. They moved in every direction. The edge of where they lived was called the *frontier*. People living on the edge were called *pioneers*.

The frontier was full of danger. Pioneers had to be tough.

Abe was born on the frontier. He grew up in a pioneer family.

Draw a Tree

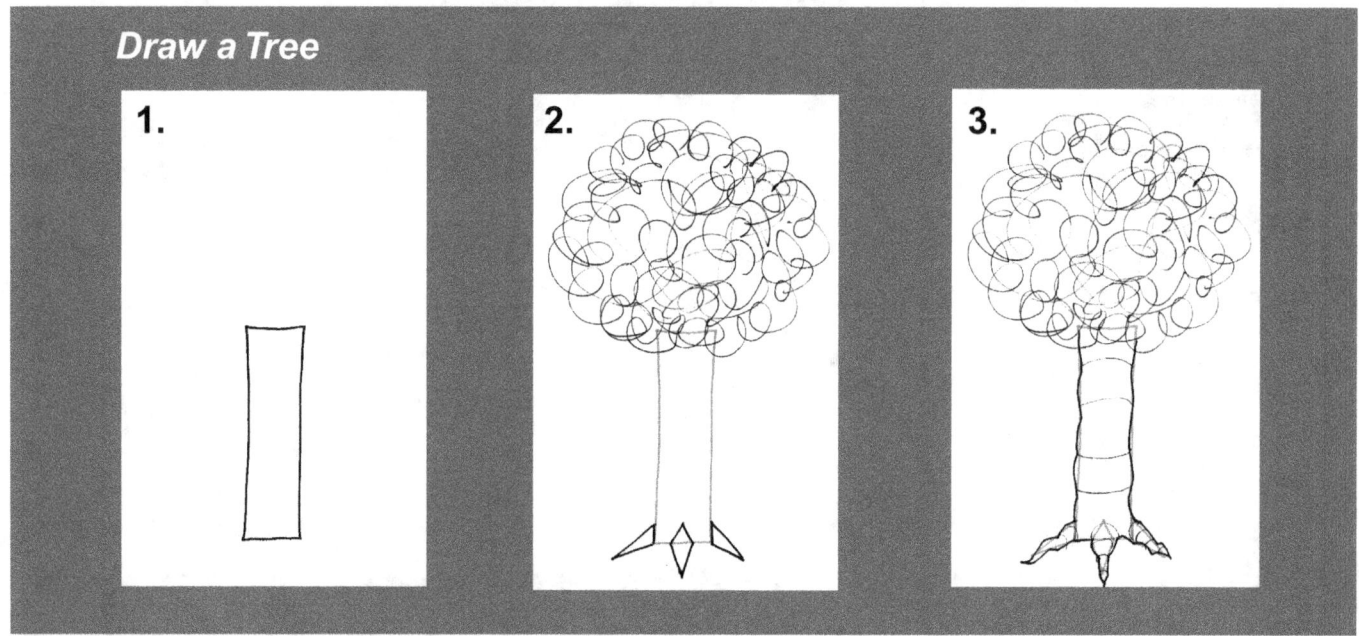

1. **2.** **3.**

Leafy shadow
Leaves make shade. We can show shade on the tree trunk.

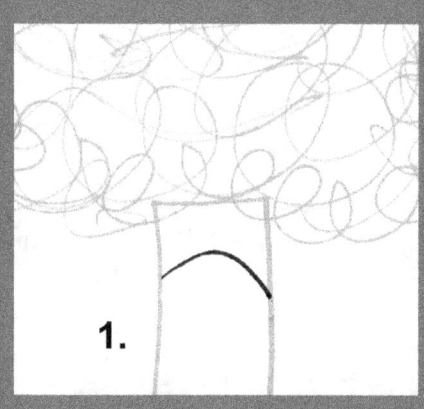

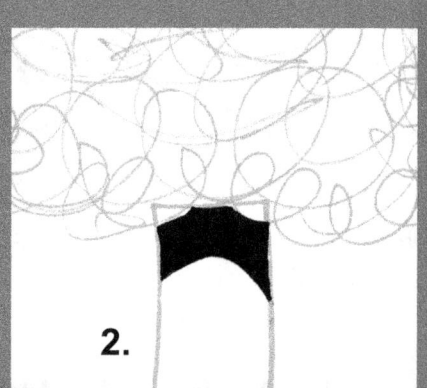

1. **2.**

Clearing farmland

Pioneers were farmers. When they settled on land, they cut down almost all the trees. Farm fields replaced forests.

Pioneers cut trees to clear land. But they also used the wood. They made buildings out of tree trunks. They burned branches to heat their homes. They burned wood to cook their food. They made wooden tools, furniture and fences.

An ax was the main tool for cutting trees.

Nature as an enemy

Today we value trees. We protect nature. But people did not always feel this way.

Pioneers thought nature was their enemy. Dark forests meant danger. Open fields meant sunshine and safety.

There were many more trees than people. Pioneers felt the supply of trees would never run out. By chopping trees, pioneers fought against Nature.

Draw a tree stump and ax

1.
2.
3.
4.

Building shelter

When moving to the frontier, pioneers built shelter first. They wanted to keep their families warm and dry. They wanted to be safe from wild animals. Most pioneers built houses using trunks of trees. They called the houses *log cabins*.

Draw a Log Cabin

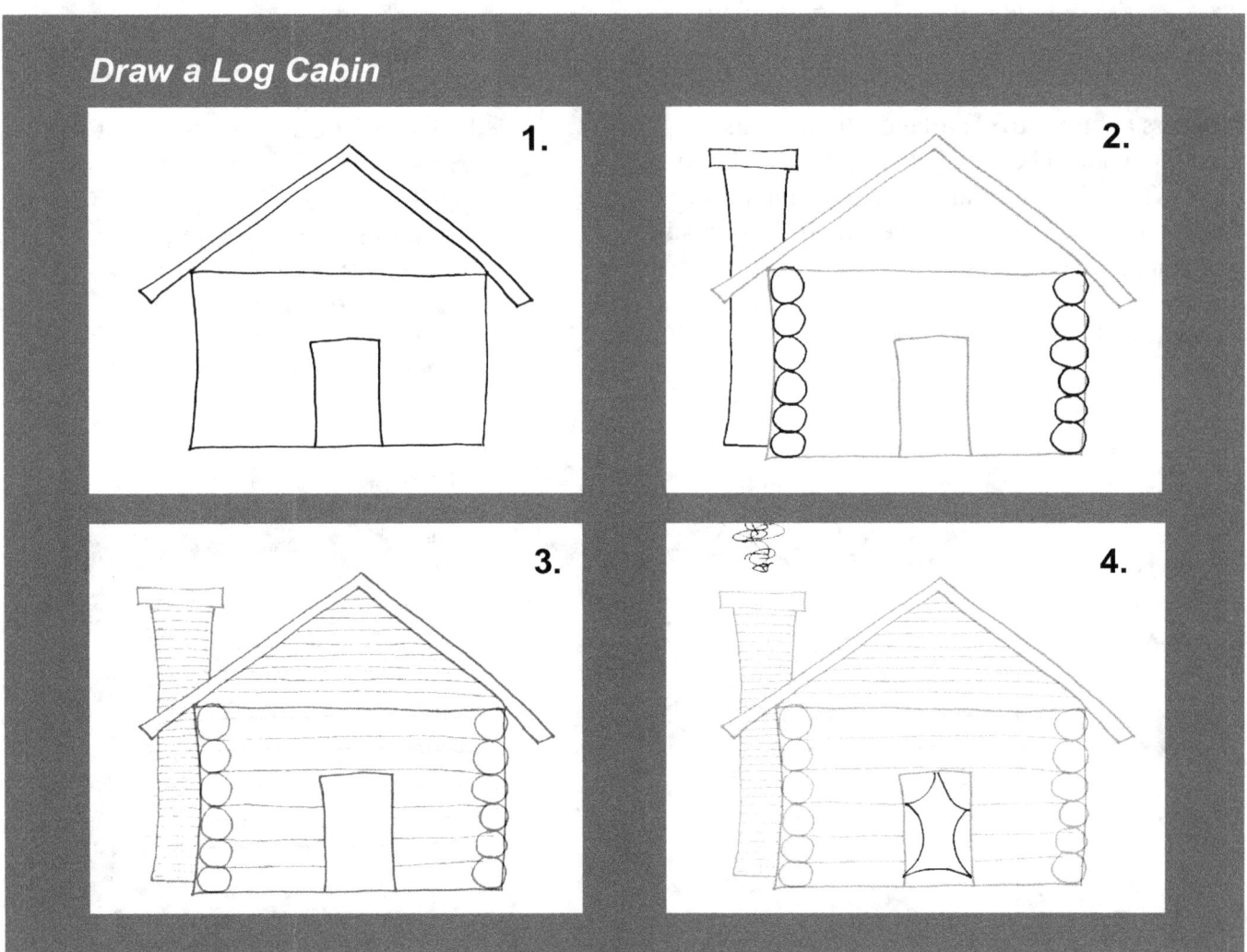

Footprint mystery

Abe's step-mother was Sarah Bush Lincoln. Sarah kept a clean house. She had the ceiling in the main room of the family's log cabin whitewashed. (Painted white.)

Abe loved a good joke. He told a young boy to step in wet mud. Then Abe tipped the boy upside down. Abe lifted him up. The boy's feet touched the ceiling. Soon dirty footprints covered the whitewash. Sarah was shocked. Someone had walked on her white ceiling!

But Sarah laughed last. Abe had to clean up the mess.

Woodland animals

Animals filled the forests of the frontier. Pioneers hunted animals for food and furs. As a boy, Abe wore a raccoon-skin hat. He wore deer-skin britches. At night, he slept under a bear-skin blanket.

But Abe had a tender heart. He did not like killing animals. As far as we know, Abe never hunted. This kindness toward animals made Abe different. He was not like other boys of his time.

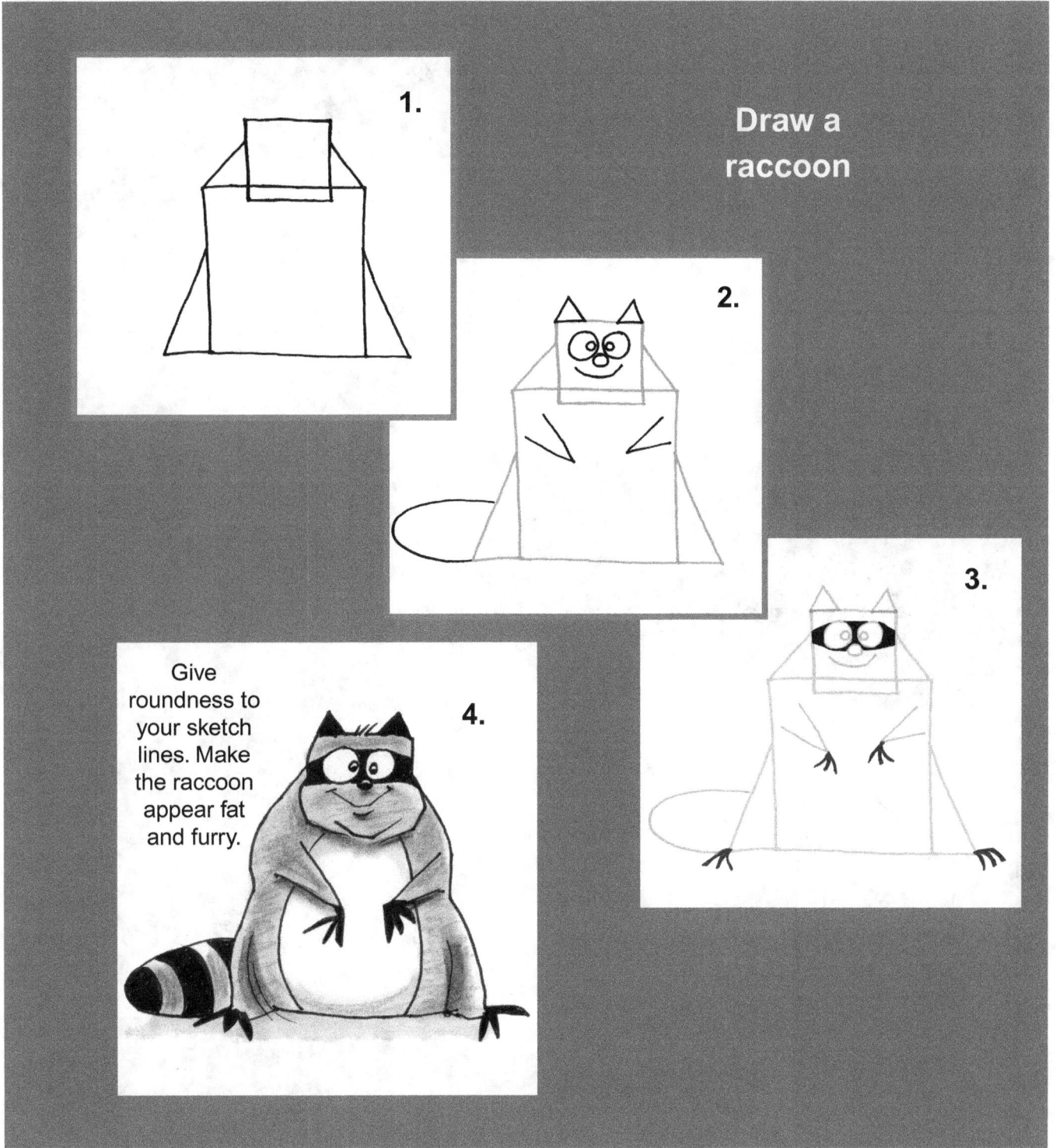

1.

Draw a raccoon

2.

3.

4.

Give roundness to your sketch lines. Make the raccoon appear fat and furry.

Supporting cast

Animal bodies are hard to draw. So we will hide these characters behind trees. Plus, this is how pioneers saw woodland animals—peeking out of the forest.

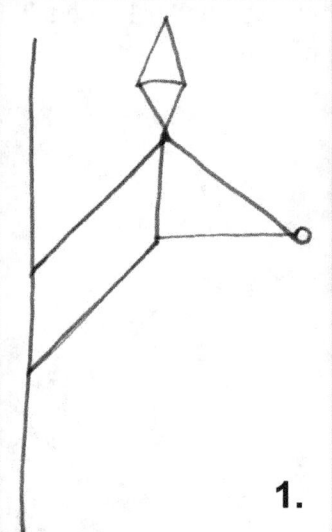

1.

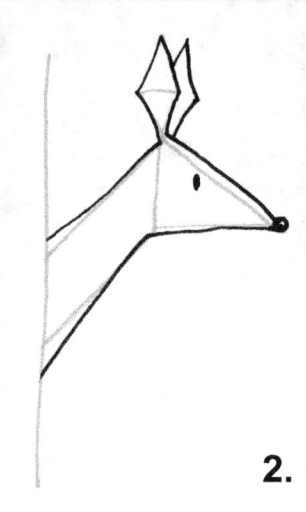

2.

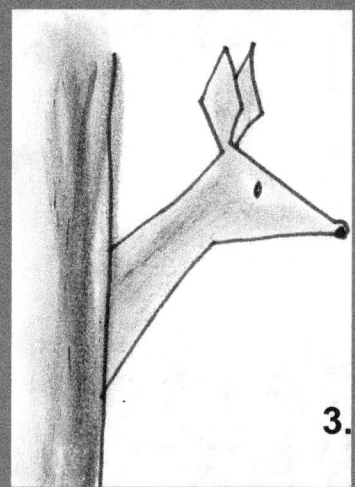

3.

Draw a deer

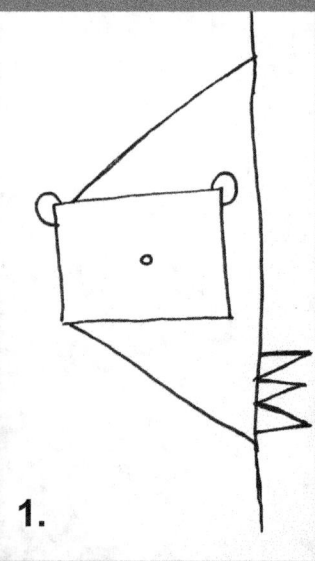

1.

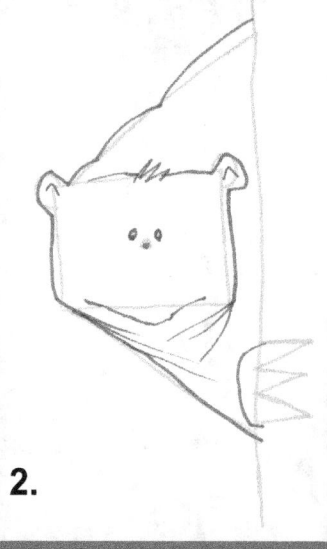

2.

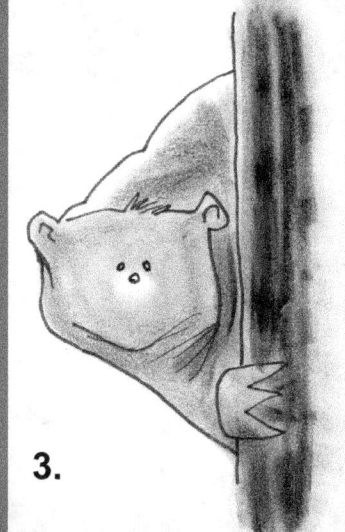

3.

Draw a bear

Draw a frontier background
Now you can draw a background for Abe's childhood!

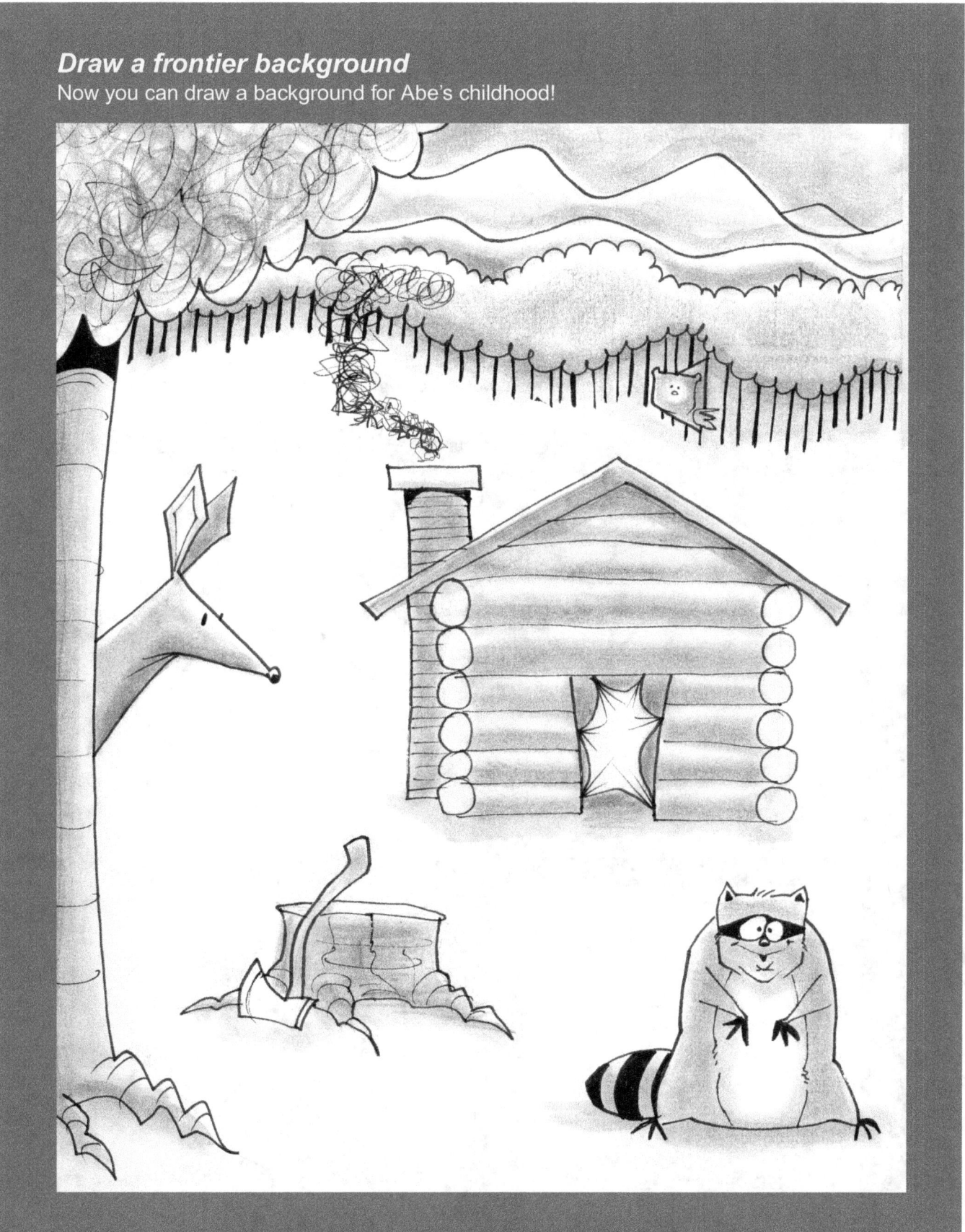

Abe's Early Years

Growing up

Pioneers worked long hours. So did young Abe. He planted pumpkin seeds between hills of corn. He carried water from a well. He gathered nuts and berries in the forest. He chopped wood for the fireplace.

Sickness and accidents stung pioneers. Many people died. Abe lost his mother and sister. His kind heart ached. Abe carried this sadness the rest of his life.

But Abe also had fun. He played jokes. He told stories. He loved to learn. He went to school only about one year, but Abe read every book he could find. And he dreamed of doing great things.

What did Abe look like as a boy? We don't know. But we can guess. The secret is simple shapes.

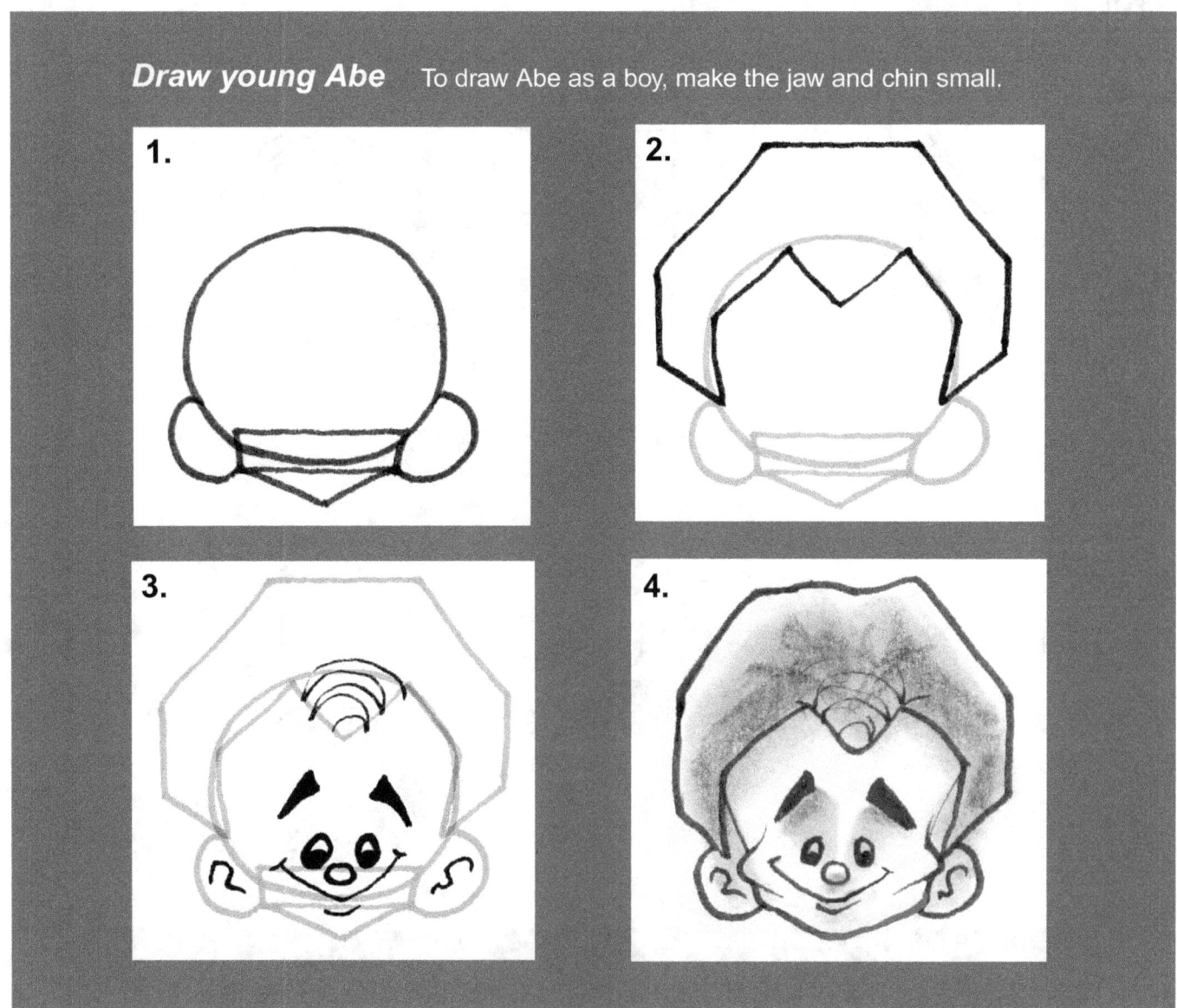

Draw young Abe To draw Abe as a boy, make the jaw and chin small.

Draw a young boy's body

1.

2.

No shoes! Abe often went barefoot.

3.

4.

Make the shirt and pants too small. Abe grew fast!

Draw a body in motion

Moving bodies are difficult to draw. This cartoon body does not use simple shapes.
But you can do it. How? Practice, practice, practice. (Continued on next page.)

1.

2.

3.

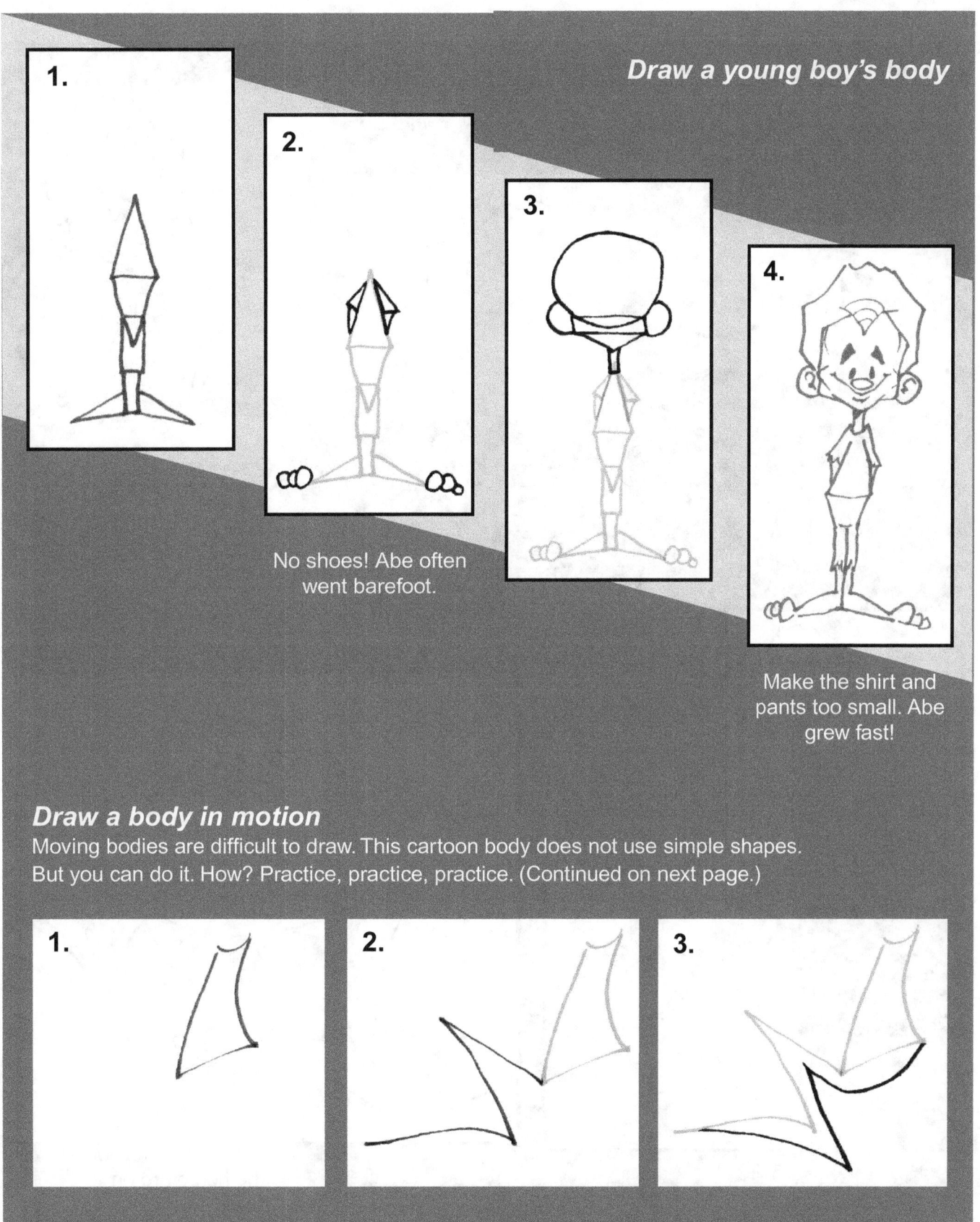

Draw body details

The cartoon body on page 15 can be used to draw young Abe in action. Just add details.

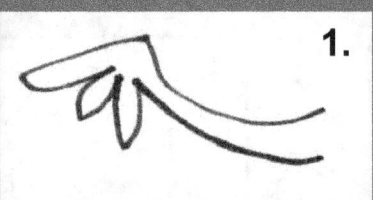

1.

Practice drawing this arm and hand.

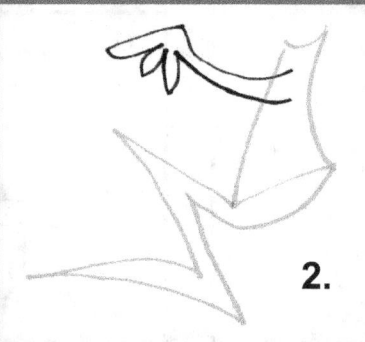

2.

Attach the arm to the seated body.

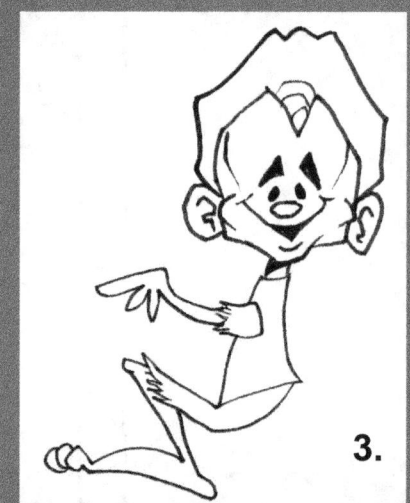

3.

Add bare feet and Abe's head.

Draw Abe in action

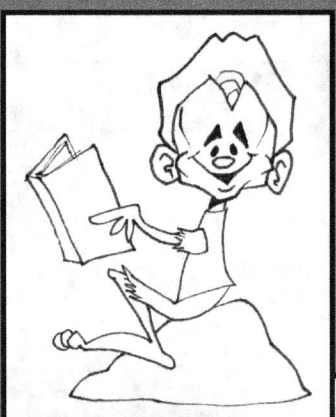

Reading . . .

. . . fishing . . .

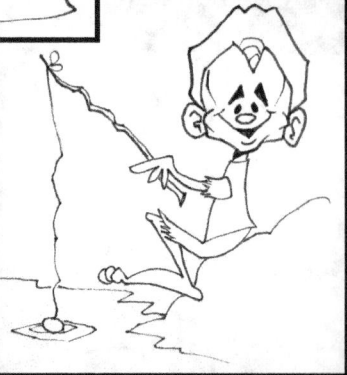

. . . horseback riding!

Directions for drawing the horse are on page 28.

Expressions

A person's face *expresses* how they feel. We call smiles, frowns and snarls *facial expressions*. An artist can show expression. Use simple shapes and lines.

Draw facial expressions

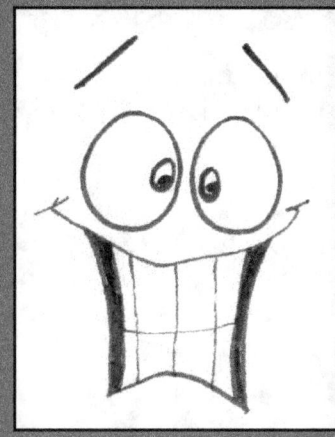

Happy

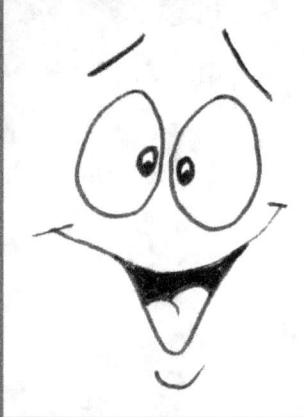

Talking

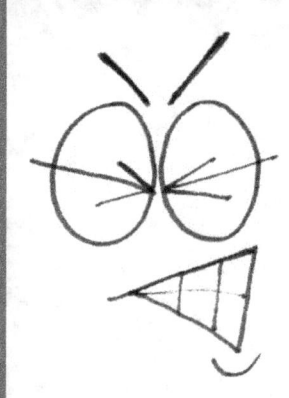

Frustration

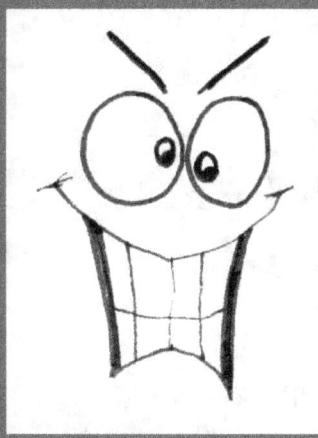

Nasty

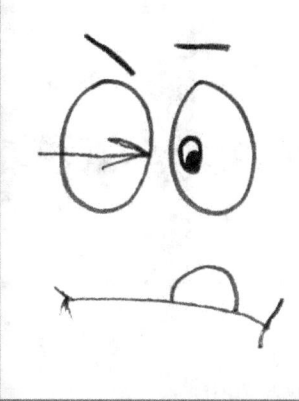

Concentrating

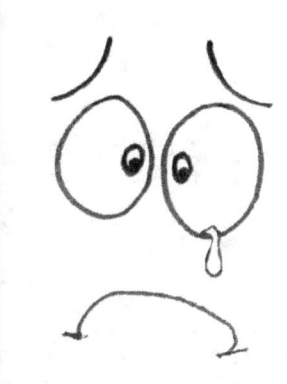

Sad

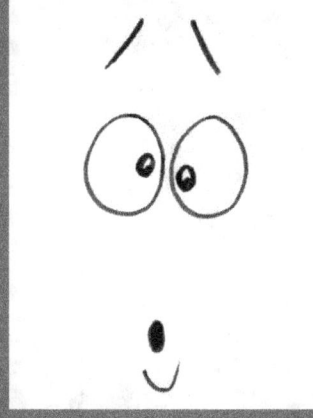

Surprise

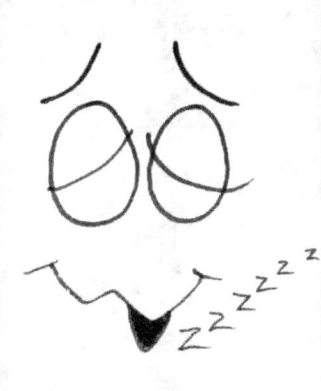

Asleep

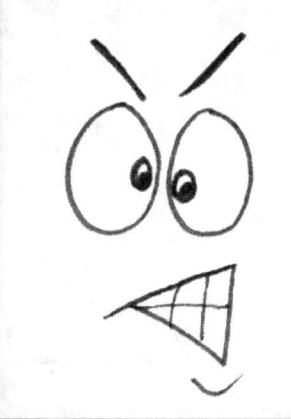

Anger

Draw a story
You now have the skills to tell stories with pictures. Try it!

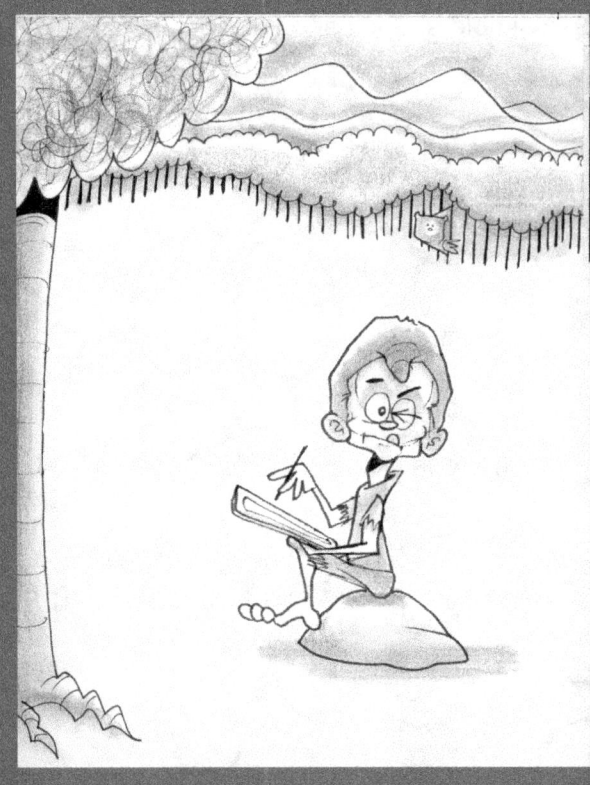
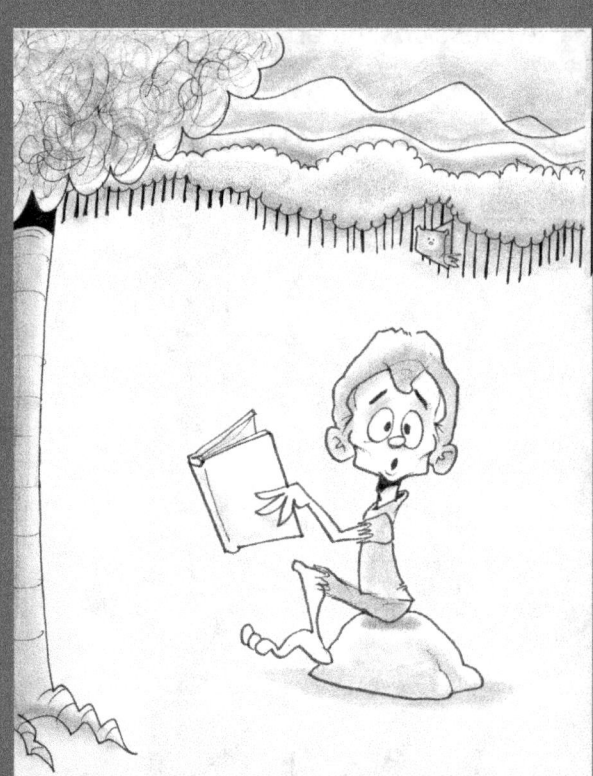
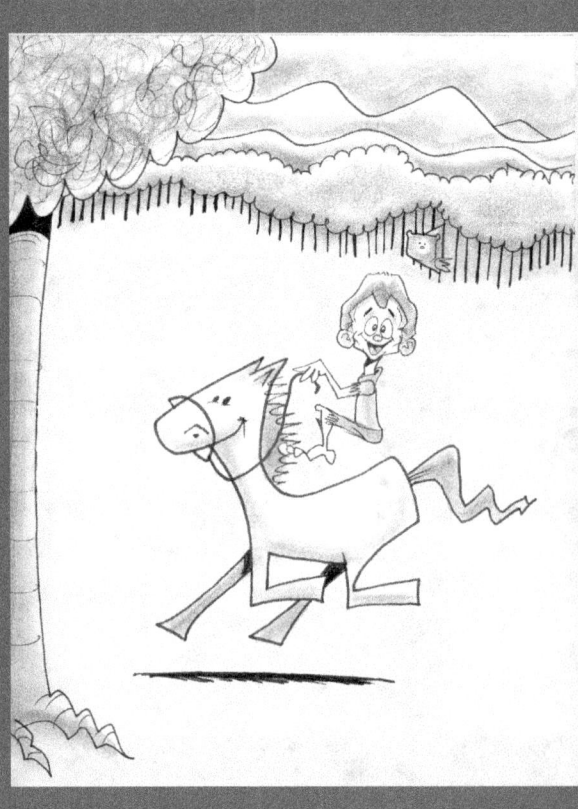
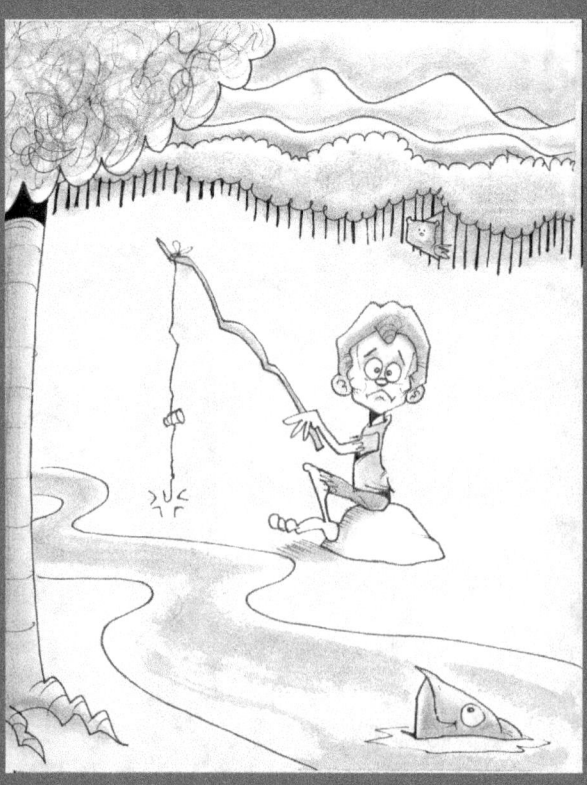

Abe as a young man

In 1830, the Lincoln family moved to Illinois. Abe moved too. But at age 21, Abe was ready to build his own life. He moved out on his own.

Abe worked many jobs. With an ax, he split logs into rails for fences. He served as a soldier. (Abe joked he only fought mosquitoes.) He stocked shelves in a general store. He steered a raft down the Mississippi River.

No matter what work he did, Abe kept learning. He read books. He practiced writing and speaking. Like the heroes in books, Abe dreamed of doing great deeds.

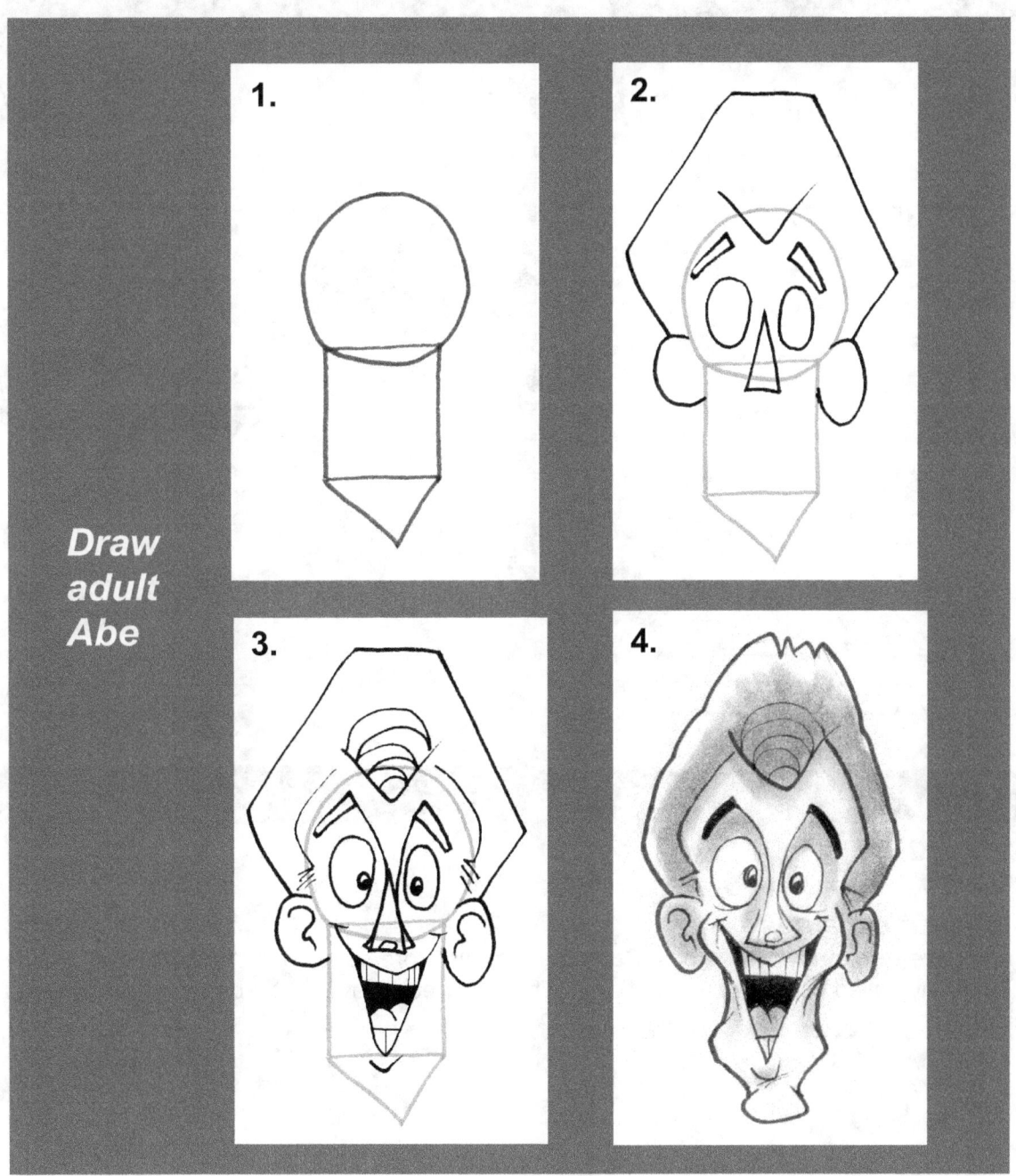

Draw adult Abe

Rail Splitter

Abe gained skill with an ax. Neighbors told how well he split logs into fence rails. Years later, Abe ran for President. Friends brought rails Abe had split to meetings. People cheered because Abe worked hard, just like them! Newspapers called Abe the "Rail Splitter." The nickname stuck.

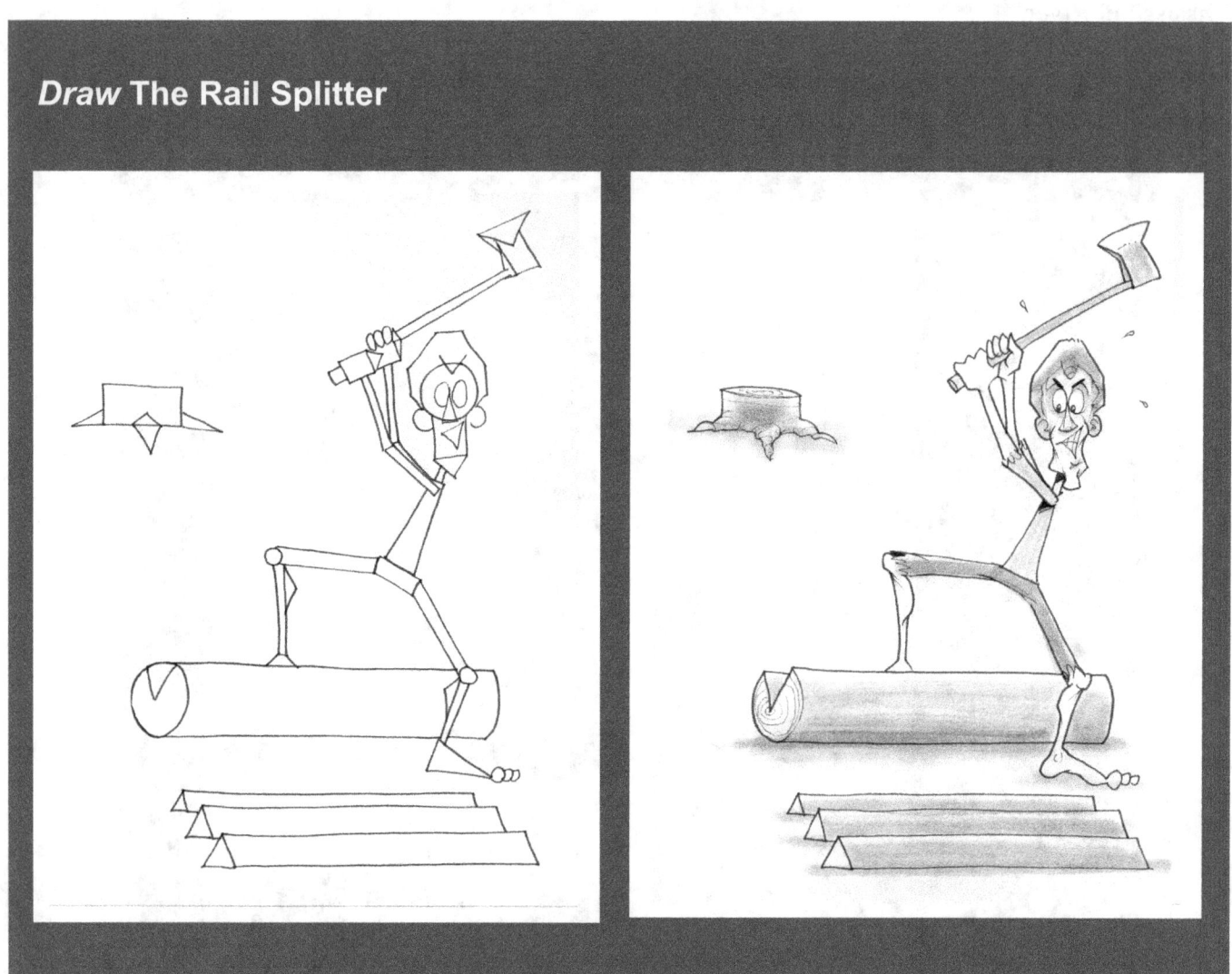

Draw The Rail Splitter

Abe's other nicknames

Americans gave Abe many nicknames. Customers of his store called him "Honest Abe." Soldiers in the U.S. Army called him "Father Abraham." When he freed slaves, Abe became "The Great Emancipator."

Stump Speaker

Abe ran for political office. He visited Illinois frontier towns. No one on the frontier owned a television, computer or video games. (Why? These things had not been invented.) Pioneers wanted politicians to entertain them. To be better heard and seen, politicians stood on tree stumps.

Draw The Stump Speaker

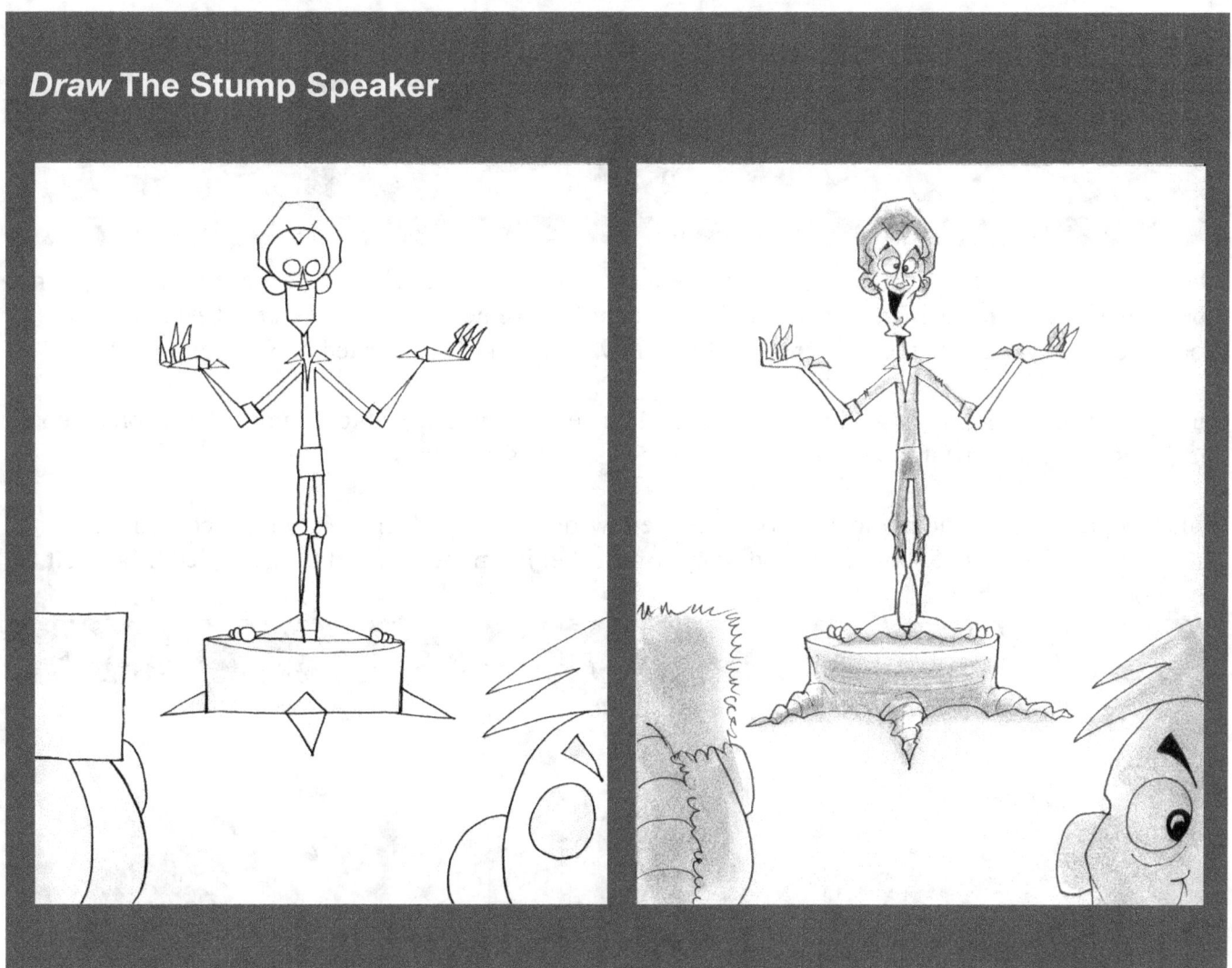

Stumping
Pioneers called politicians "stump speakers." The term is still used today. Politicians still visit small towns. They still give lots of speeches. Americans call this "stumping" for office.

Abe falls in love

When Abe moved to Springfield, Illinois, he met Mary Todd. Mary was pretty, funny and smart. Many young men fell in love with Mary. Abe fell for Mary, too.

Draw Mary Todd

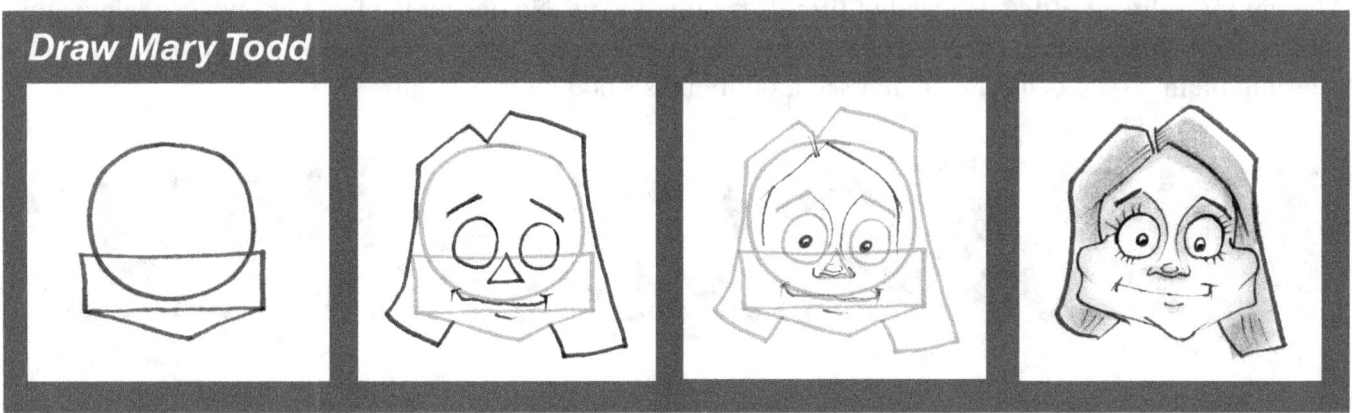

Abe and Mary could not have been more different. Abe was tall, Mary short. Abe was thin, Mary plump. Abe grew up poor and learned on his own. Mary's family gave her fine things and the best education money could buy. Despite their differences, love grew. Abe and Mary married November 4, 1842.

During their marriage, Mary got into trouble. She lost her temper. She spoke meanly. She ignored people she did not like. She spent too much money on carpets, dishes and furniture.

Some people said Abe did not love Mary. They were wrong. Abe felt lucky Mary married him. She made him angry, but he got over his anger. And Mary loved Abe. From the moment they married, Mary felt Abe would one day be president.

Draw Mary Lincoln

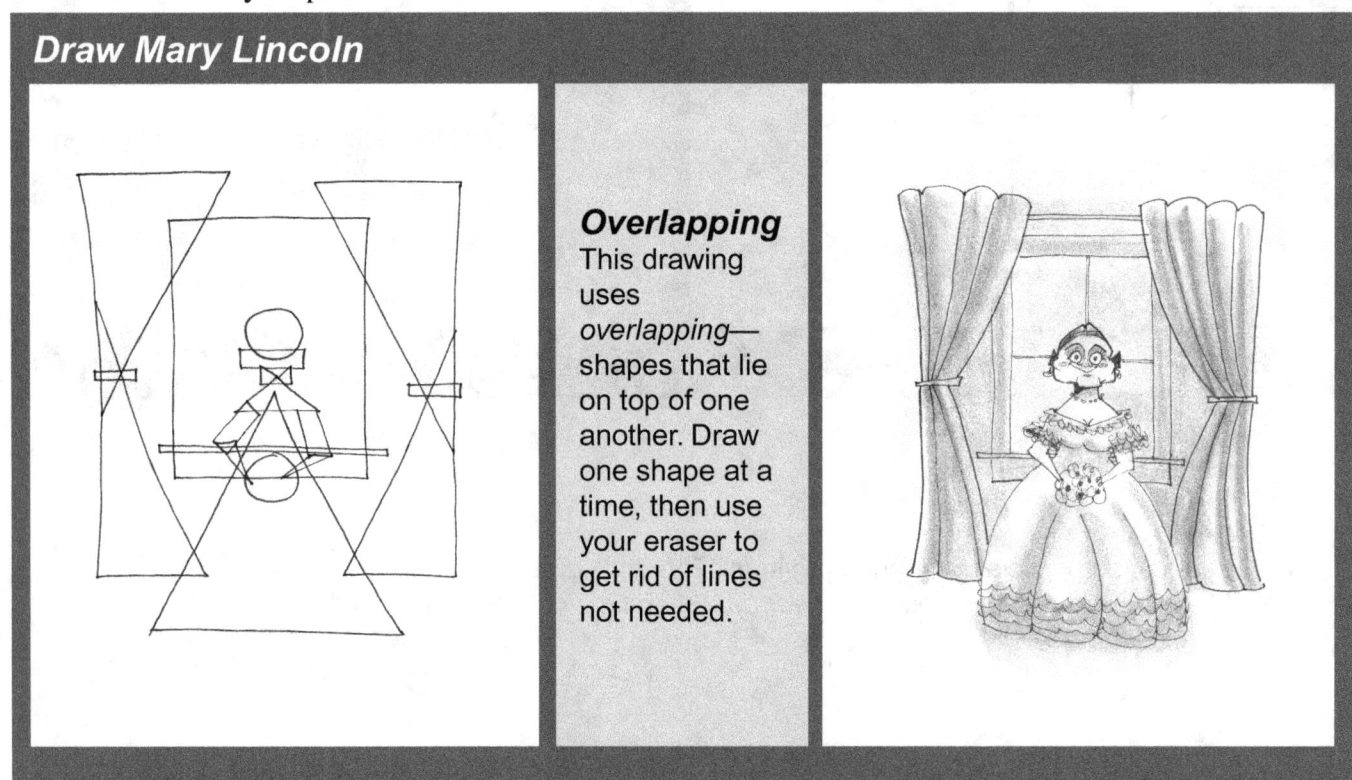

Overlapping
This drawing uses *overlapping*— shapes that lie on top of one another. Draw one shape at a time, then use your eraser to get rid of lines not needed.

Abe as president

The Great Debates

Abe felt he had failed. He put time and effort into politics for no pay. His work as a lawyer suffered. To make a better living for his family, Abe quit politics.

But Abe listened to arguments over slavery. An Illinois politician claimed states had power to decide. If a state wanted to allow slavery, it could. The politician's name was Stephen Douglas.

Draw Stephen Douglas

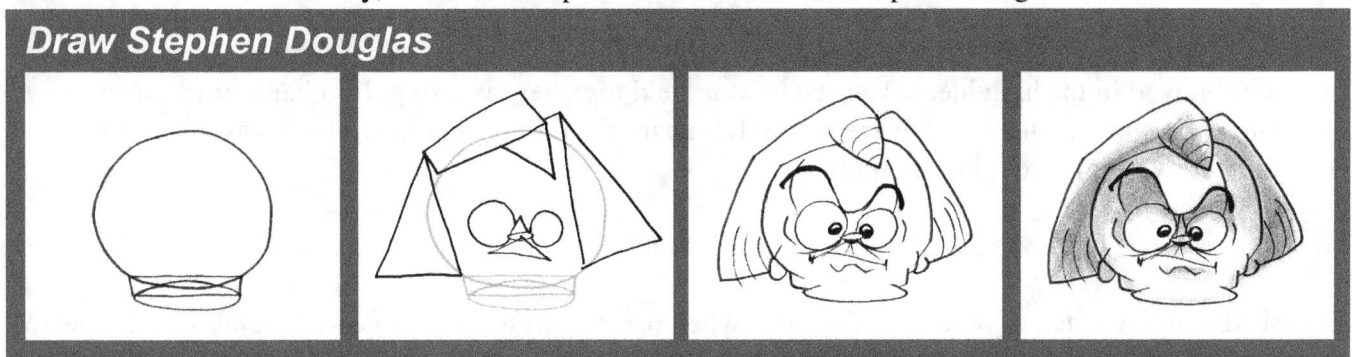

Abe was shocked. If people believed Stephen, states without slavery could change their minds! Slavery might grow. Abe felt slavery should wither and die. He believed the United States government should have more power than states. The nation should decide about slavery.

Stephen ran for senator. Abe did not want Stephen to win. Abe entered the race. Arguments between Stephen and Abe became famous. They were called *The Great Debates.*

People liked Abe. He used words they understood. He joked about himself. In a debate, Stephen called Abe "two faced." In other words, a liar! Abe knew people did not find him handsome. So he said, "If I am two-faced, would I wear the face I have now?" The crowd laughed.

Draw a debate

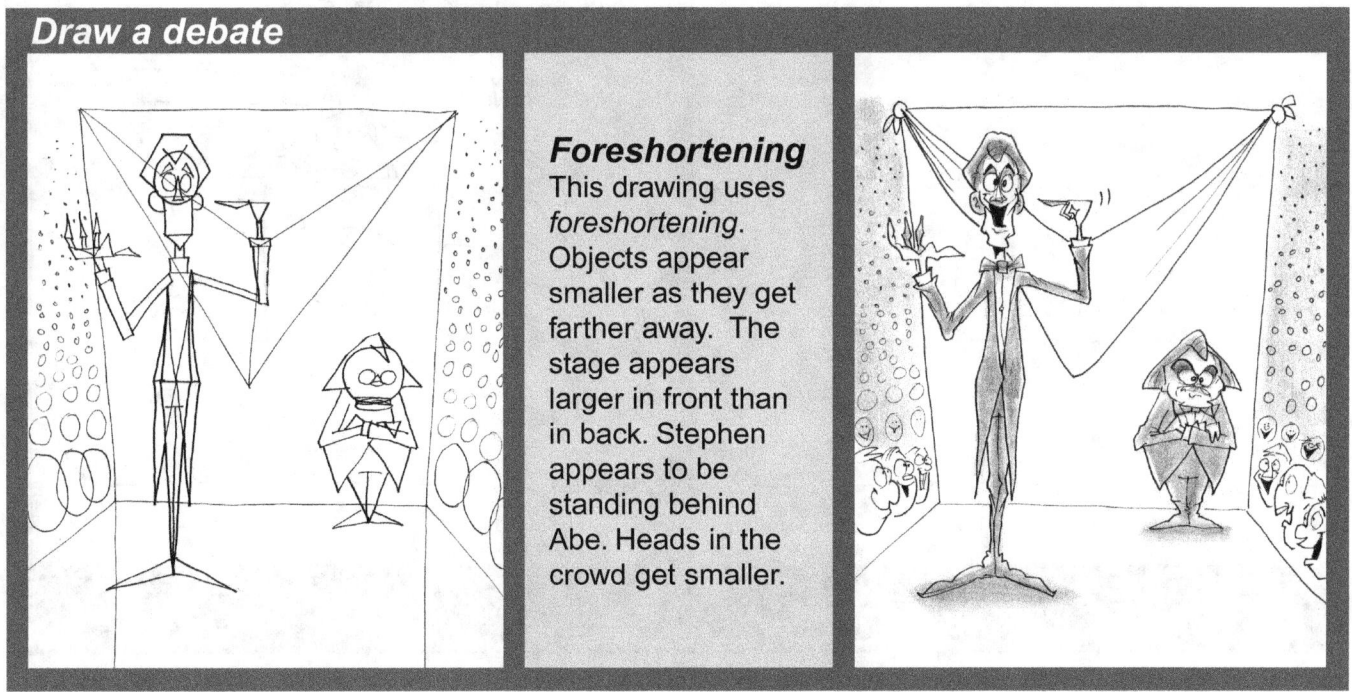

Foreshortening
This drawing uses *foreshortening.* Objects appear smaller as they get farther away. The stage appears larger in front than in back. Stephen appears to be standing behind Abe. Heads in the crowd get smaller.

The election of 1860

The Great Debates made Abe famous. Abe lost the Senate race, but he won respect. People who hated slavery admired the Rail Splitter. In 1860, the nation elected Abe president.

But the nation was sick and weak. The United States had been built on high ideas. One idea said "All men are created equal." But some states allowed slavery. How could a nation with high ideas allow slavery? It could not. Either the high ideas or slavery had to go.

As soon as Abe was elected, some states left the nation. These states felt they had the right to decide. But Abe believed in the high ideas. The states were held together by voting. In other words, *government by the people*. United. One union. If the nation fell apart when states got mad, there was no union. Government by voting would be a failure.

The Civil War began. It was a scary time in United States history.

At first Abe only wanted to save the union. But when the war grew, he changed his mind. It was time to fix the problem. It was time for the nation to act on its high ideas. Abe ended slavery in the United States. The paper that ended slavery was called *The Emancipation Proclamation*.

Draw The Great Emancipator

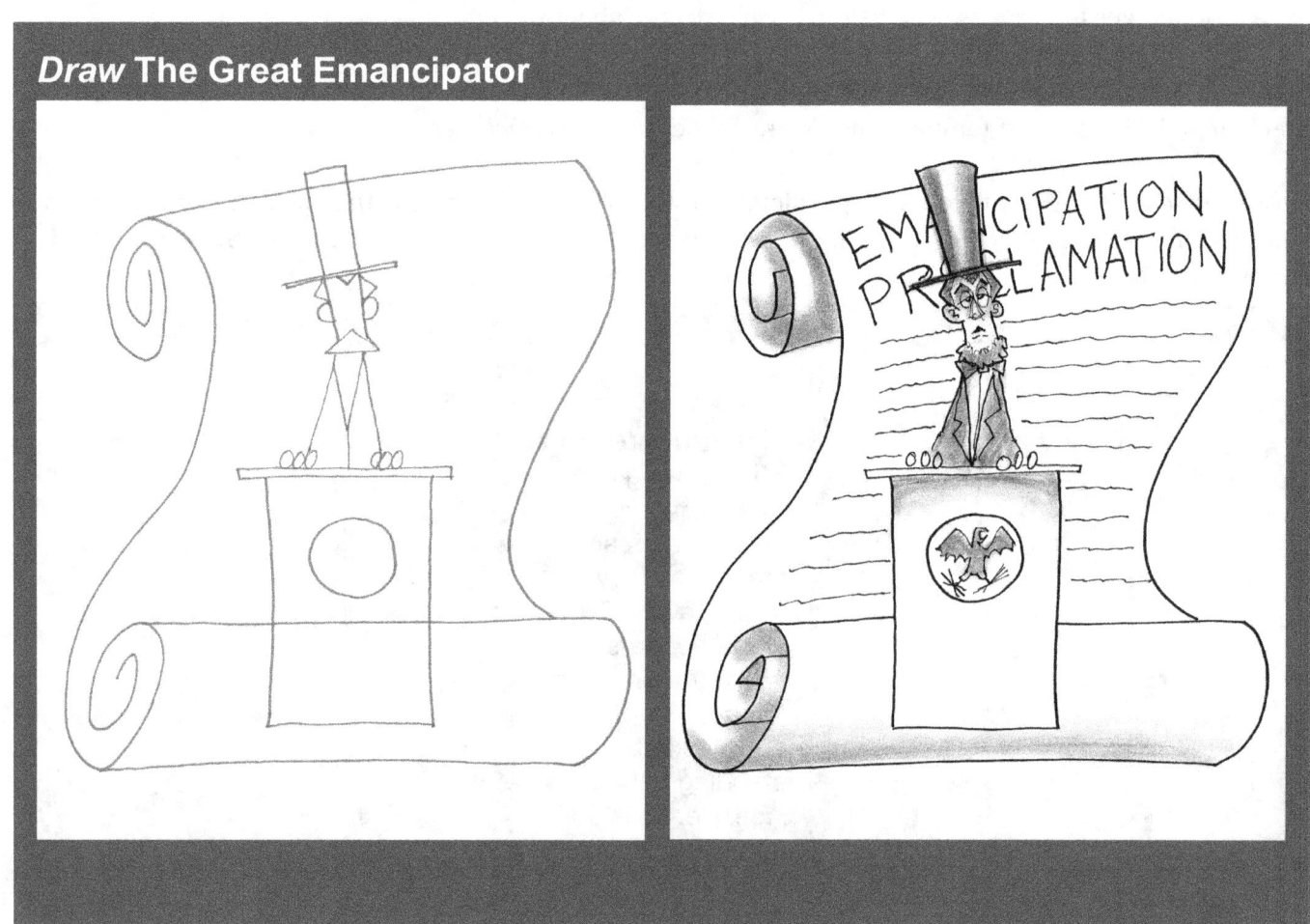

Changing and growing

Most people consider Abe the greatest president. He could change his mind and grow.

Abe listened to everyone. He thought about all arguments before making up his mind. He acted at just the right time.

Abe thought a lot about slavery. He thought masters should be paid to set slaves free. He thought former slaves should be shipped to Africa. Abe did not think former slaves could be happy in the United States. Then Abe met Frederick Douglass.

Born a slave, Frederick served several masters. One master's wife taught Frederick to read. Reading opened a new world to Frederick—a world of ideas. Frederick read the high ideas that built the United States. He thought about slavery. Frederick knew he was as good as any man. Why was he beaten? Why was he forced to give money he earned to his master? Slavery was not fair.

Frederick could not stand unfairness. He ran away. He settled down with a wife. He got a job. But the unfairness of slavery still bothered him.

Frederick went to meetings of people who wanted to end slavery. The people asked Frederick to speak. His life story moved them. Other groups asked Frederick to speak. Finally, Frederick wrote his life story. People across the nation read his book. Frederick became famous.

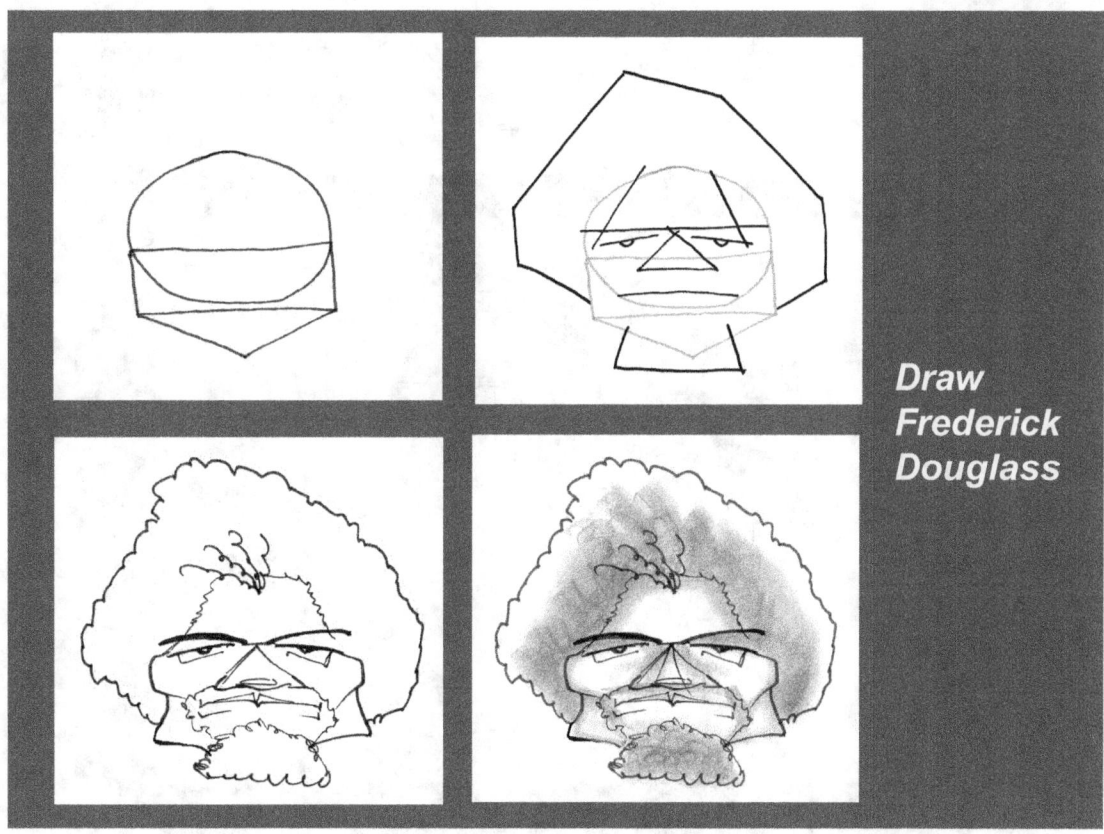

Draw Frederick Douglass

Frederick and Abe became friends. Frederick told Abe former slaves did not want to go to Africa. They had been born in the United States. This was their country, too. Former slaves only wanted to be treated fairly. They wanted the United States to live up to its high ideas.

Abe changed his mind. He dropped plans to pay masters. He dropped plans to ship former slaves to Africa. He began plans for former slaves and masters to live together.

Abe did not live to carry out the plans. Just as the war was ending, a man shot Abe. Abe died April 15, 1865.

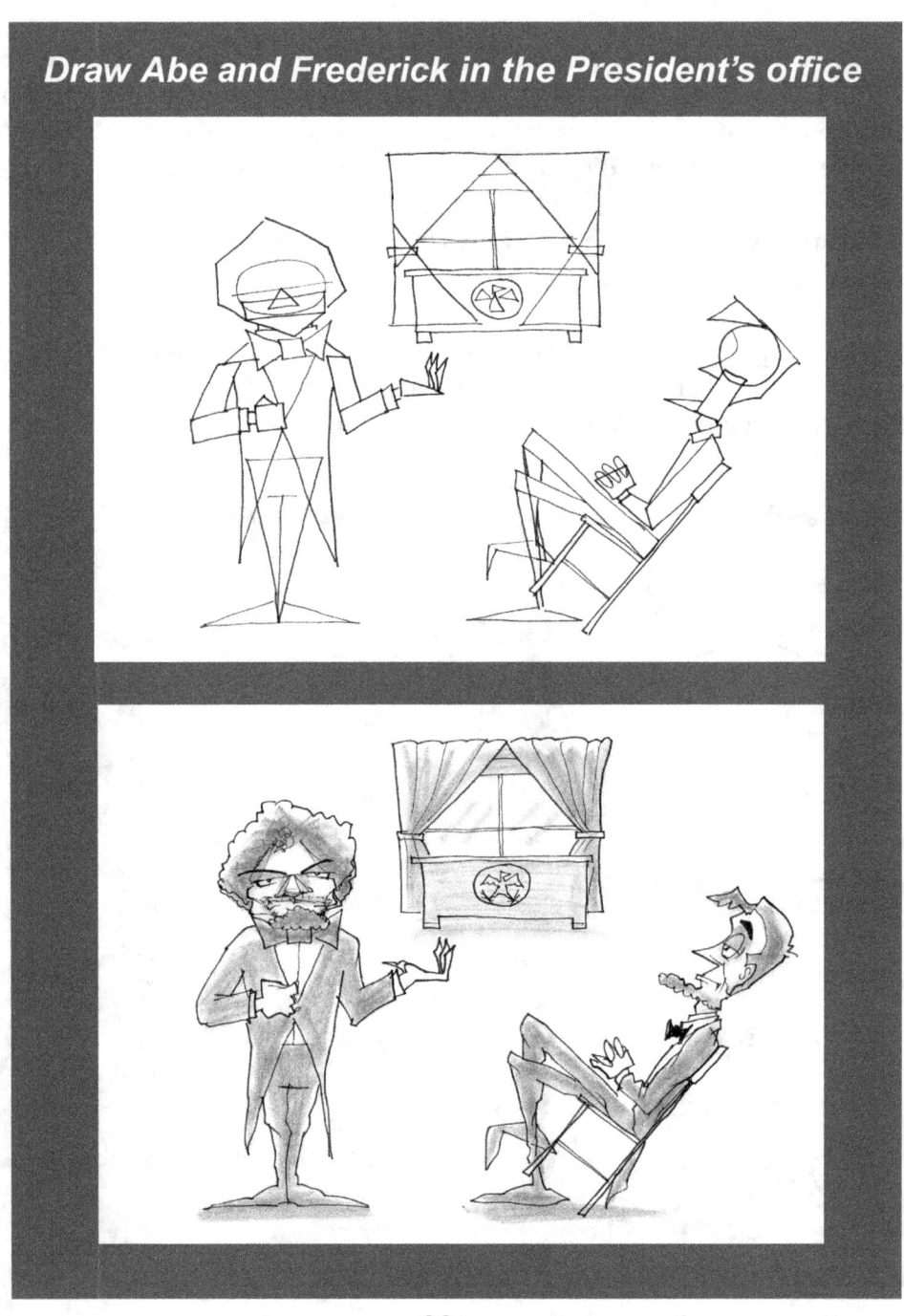

Draw Abe and Frederick in the President's office

Abe's ideas still live. Abe called the Civil War *a new birth of freedom*. Like birth, the war was painful. Like birth, the war gave the nation new life. The United States took its first steps up a steep road—the road to high ideas.

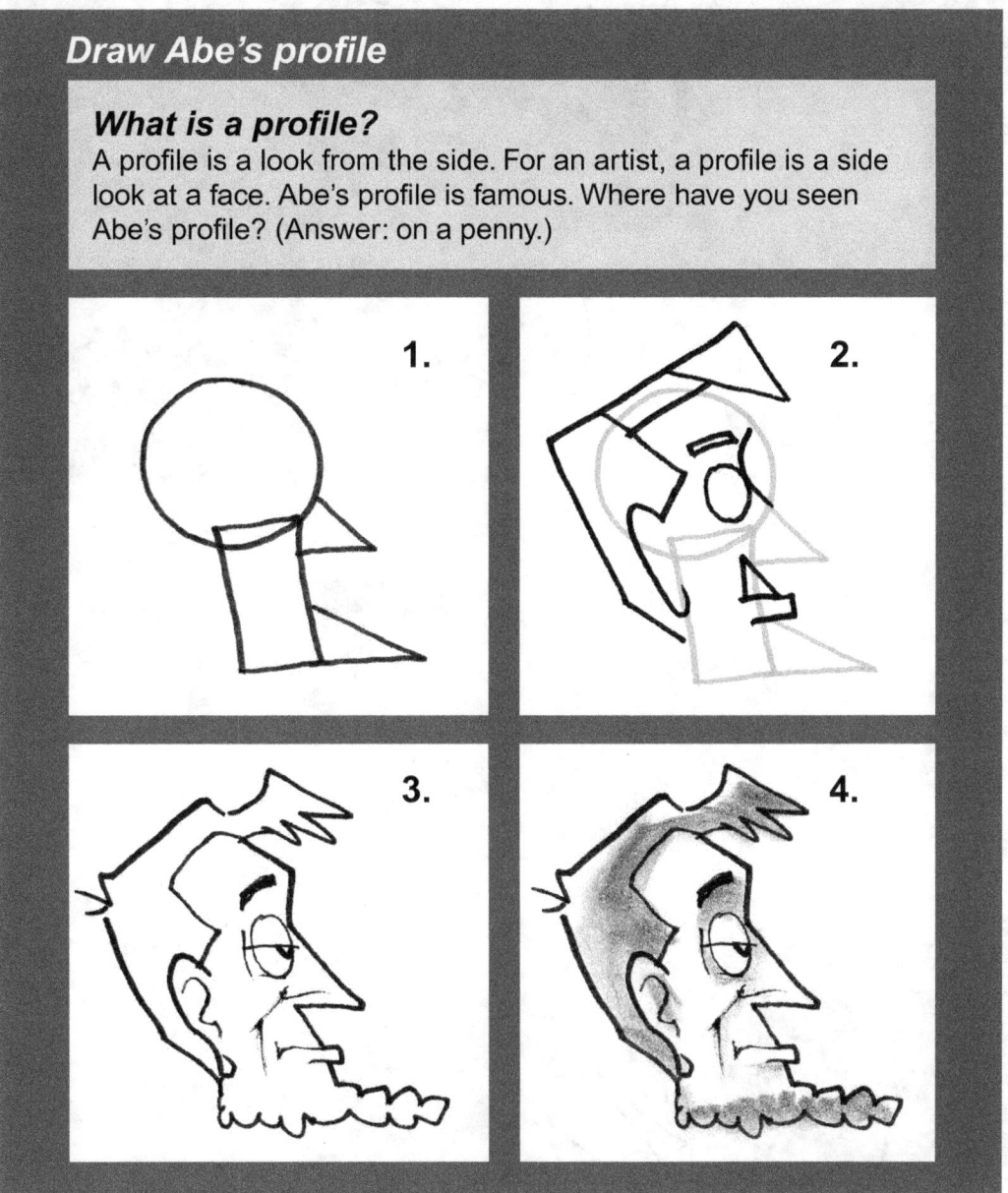

Draw Abe's profile

What is a profile?
A profile is a look from the side. For an artist, a profile is a side look at a face. Abe's profile is famous. Where have you seen Abe's profile? (Answer: on a penny.)

The Path Ahead

You have made it to the end of an amazing story. A poor boy becomes president. A weak nation grows strong. New life comes out of a bloody war.

You have just started work as an artist. Where will you go from here? Like Abe and Frederick, will you learn on your own? Will you change and grow?

The ending is up to you.

Draw a Cartoon Horse

Here is how to draw the horse on page 19. This drawing is difficult. It does not use simple shapes. It uses related lines. Only through practice can you expect good results.

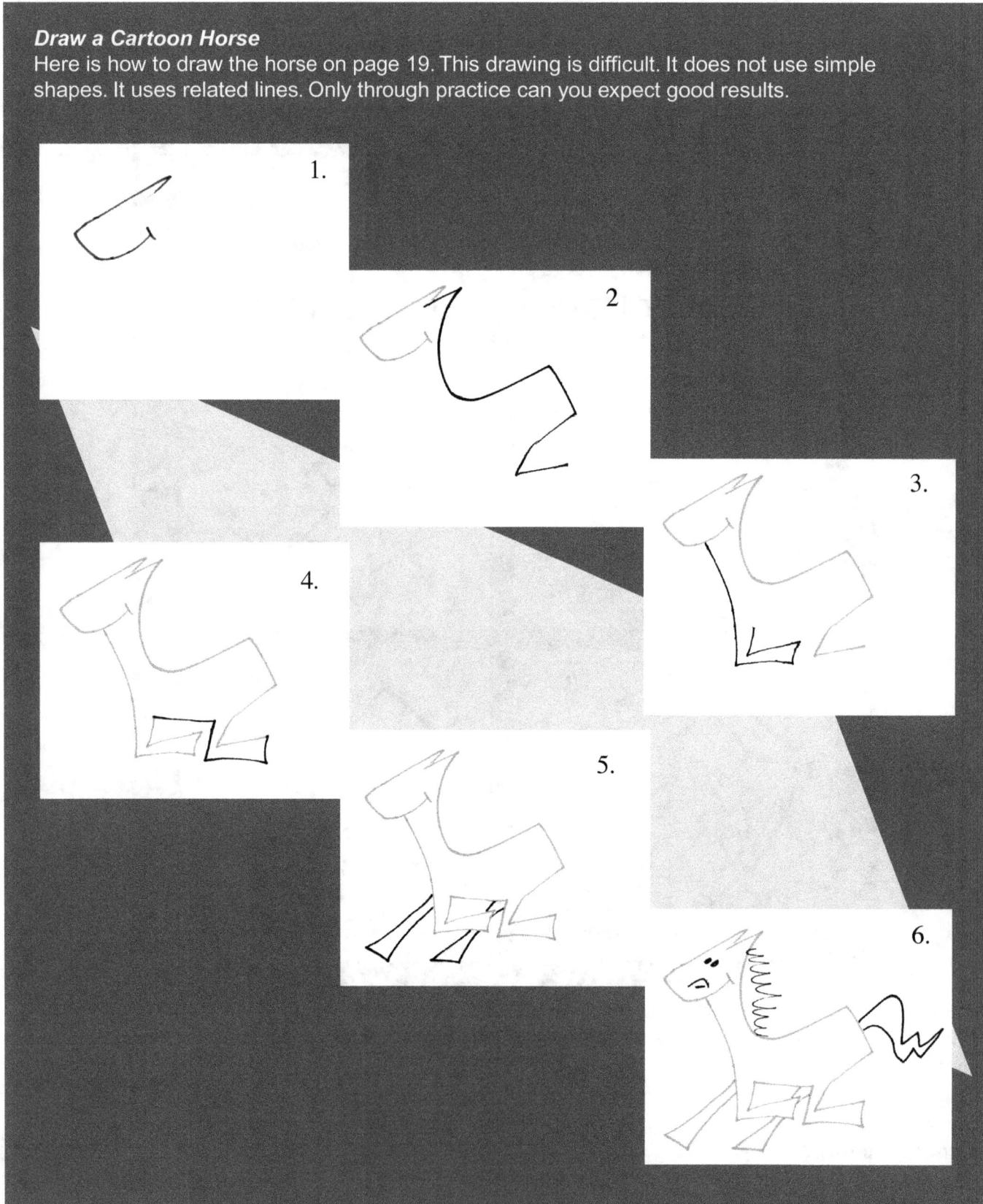